# ENGAGING SCRIPTURE

*Reading the Bible
with Early Friends*

**By Michael L. Birkel**

Foreword by M. Basil Pennington, ocso

*Friends* United Press
and
Earlham Press

Richmond, Indiana

Copyright 2005 by Michael L. Birkel.

We express gratitude to Earlham College and its Newlin Center for Quaker Thought and Practice for support of this book through the Project on Spiritual Formation: Faith, Vocation, and Leadership, funded by the Lilly Endowment's Program for the Theological Exploration of Vocation.

    Library of Congress Cataloging-in-Publication Data

    Birkel, Michael Lawrence.
      Engaging Scripture : reading the Bible with early Friends / by Michael L. Birkel ; foreword by M. Basil Pennington.
        p. cm.
      Includes bibliographical references and index.
      ISBN 0-944350-67-4 (alk. paper)
      1. Bible-Devotional use-History. 2. Spirituality-Society of Friends-History. I. Title.
      BX7738.B56 2005
      220.6'088'2896-dc22
                                                  2005047894

To my father, Francis Birkel, who showed me a deep love of reading during my childhood and in more recent years has been a conversation partner on the spiritual life.

Thanks.

*Filius sapiens doctrina patris audit. (Proverbs 13:1)*

# Contents

Acknowledgments . . . . . . . . . . . . . . . . . . . . . . . . . . . . vii

Foreword . . . . . . . . . . . . . . . . . . . . . . . . . . . . . . . . . . . . . ix
    M. Basil Pennington, ocso

Introduction: Reading in Company . . . . . . . . . . . . . . xv

One: Reading Inwardly . . . . . . . . . . . . . . . . . . . . . . . . . 1

Two: Reading and Remembering . . . . . . . . . . . . . . . . 13

Three: Reading Meditatively . . . . . . . . . . . . . . . . . . . . 25

Four: Reading Together . . . . . . . . . . . . . . . . . . . . . . . . 41

Five: Reading with the Wider Church . . . . . . . . . . . . 49

Six: Reading to Be Transformed . . . . . . . . . . . . . . . . . 65

Appendices
    A. More Reading with Early Friends . . . . . . . . . . 75
    B. Questions for Reflection and Journaling . . . 95

Endnotes . . . . . . . . . . . . . . . . . . . . . . . . . . . . . . . . . . . 109

Scripture Index . . . . . . . . . . . . . . . . . . . . . . . . . . . . . . 119

# Acknowledgments

This book is a harvest that has been several years in the making. I explored some of these ideas in a seminar at Earlham College, and I am particularly grateful to three of the students in that course: Kevin O'Brien, Heather Craigie, and Sara Patek Marean. I have been invited to speak or lead workshops or retreats with a variety of Friends from Pendle Hill westward through Lake Erie, Ohio Valley, Wilmington, Indiana, and Western Yearly Meetings on the subject of how early Friends engaged with scripture. Their kind reception persuaded me that Friends might find a book like this useful. A much briefer treatment of George Fox's *Epistle 227* appeared in my *Silence and Witness*, and an earlier look at Dorothy White's *Trumpet* came out in *Quaker Religious Thought*. I am thankful to those who read and commented on all or portions of the emerging manuscript: Gwen Halsted, Mary Garman, Stephanie Ford, Stephen Angell, Sue Kern, and Francis Birkel. I owe a special debt to Sue Kern and Dortha Meredith at the Newlin Center for Quaker Thought and Practice at Earlham College. Through their initiative, the publication of this book is a collaboration between Friends United Press and Earlham College.

Thank you, Dortha and Sue. Once again, I am much indebted to Barbara Mays, whose ministry of editing has improved this book in numerous ways. I am also grateful to M. Basil Pennington, ocso, for his kind and thoughtful Foreword. Thanks to him, a direct descendant of Isaac Penington, this volume is graced with bookends from the mystical Penington family.

# Foreword

This is a beautiful book that Michael Birkel has given us, especially for those of us from the Quaker tradition but for all Christian sisters and brothers. How good it is to touch the spirit or be touched by the spirit of these great forebears. In a very special way they put us in touch with the great living Christian tradition and with one of the very enriching practices in it.

In 1996, the Trappist Abbey of Gethsemani hosted a gathering of Buddhist and Christian monastics. Spiritual teachers from each tradition spent a week in fruitful dialogue, sharing the spiritual riches of their heritage. In reporting on the meeting in the Buddhist journal, *The Snow Lion*, a Buddhist monk said that among all the wonderful things shared during that week the teaching he found most profitable was the Christian way of reading their sacred texts, especially in a talk on *lectio divina* given by a Benedictine nun.* He felt this offered a way in which Buddhists could more fruitfully and effectively approach their own sacred texts.

Christians treasure their sacred scriptures. They see the Bible as inspired by God and a place to encounter God in his Word. But Christianity is not monolithic;

there is a rich diversity to be found within the Christian community. I would dare say there are few, perhaps even among the Friends, who have had an opportunity to be enriched by what the early Friends offer us in regard to this essential part of our common tradition.

As Michael Birkel well brings out, these graced men and women were very much in line with the traditional practice of the early Church fathers and the great Cistercian monastic fathers of the Middle Age. There was a significant shift in the later twelfth century, which had begun already in the tenth century but was clearly set forth by Guigo the Carthusian, whom Michael Birkel presents. Guigo saw the approach to prayerful reading in four distinct steps: reading the text, discursively meditating on it, responding to it in affective prayer, and finally resting in the reality in contemplation. One of the dangers of this more rationalistic approach to sacred reading is that we tended to squeeze the inspired Word into our narrow concepts rather than letting it expand our perception beyond our held limits. This led to a general loss of the contemplative dimension of prayer and life where we are awed by what we cannot comprehend.

As we see in Michael Birkel's work, the approach of the early Quakers was very much that of the earlier patristic tradition, a sapiential approach, which allows the inspired Word to form our minds and hearts. Like the early Fathers they did not seek to develop their teaching in some strictly logical or discursive order but allowed one inspired Word to call forth another by association, enriching and expanding their understanding.

Another facet of sacred reading that Michael Birkel found among these early Quaker writers is the rich use of the imagination to enter into the inspired Word and draw out from it an impact on their present-day living. This powerful imaginative approach was explicitly developed and set forth a century earlier by Saint Ignatius, the founder of the Jesuits, in his classical *Spiritual Exercises*. One can wonder if these early Friends did not find among their cellmates some of the equally persecuted Jesuits.

What I find most striking among the enriching ideas that Michael Birkel brings forward in regard to sacred reading is the idea of reading with these spiritual mothers and fathers. It is as though when we sit down to meet the Lord in his revealed Word we invite this Friend of old to join us as a sort of third party in the conversation. The author does extol the value of group lectio where each is enriched by what the Spirit leads other members of the group to share from their experience of God in the Word. But when we cannot be with a group, we do not need to go alone. We can invite a father of old, like Saint Augustine, or one of the Cistercian masters, such as Bernard of Clairvaux, or one of the wise and saintly Friends whom Michael Birkel introduces.

For me, another striking note in meeting these early Friends is how frequently they draw their inspiration from the Song of Songs, undoubtedly one of the most contemplative and mystic portions of the inspired Word. This was certainly a favorite book of the Cistercian fathers of the twelfth century who never ceased to draw inspiration from it.

When I come to sacred reading I make sure to do five things:

*Come into Presence*: I want to be profoundly aware that the Lord is indeed present to me in his inspired word.

*Call upon the Spirit*: I seek the help of Holy Spirit. At the Last Supper Jesus assured us that the Spirit, the Paraclete, would teach us all things, call to mind all he taught us.

*Listen:* Here the wonderful spiritual forebears to whom Michael introduces us can indeed help us to learn this sacred art of a wide-open, totally receptive, sapiential listening.

*Thank*: At the end of this wondrous meeting with the Lord in his Word, I want to thank the Divine for being so graciously condescending as to give this intimate time even to this least of his creatures.

*Take a Word*: As I move forward into my day of service I want to take a word (word, phrase or sentence) from our meeting, which I allow to abide in my spirit and repeat itself in my mind to constantly renew my communion with the Presence.

How much, in these harried times of ours, do we need the contemplative space to enter into the meeting house of the scriptures and in an unhurried way amble through the garden of Wisdom and taste and see and be refreshed. Engrossed in this inner landscape we can truly find peace and be a source of peace for others and for the whole of this poor world of ours, which we come to hold in infinitely tender care.

M. Basil Pennington, ocso

*[Ed. Note: Interested readers can find the presentation by Mary Margaret Funk, O.S.B. in *The Gethesemani Encounter: A Dialogue on the Spiritual Life By Buddhist and Christian Monastics*, edited by Donald W. Mitchell and James Wiseman, O.S.B. (New York: Continuum, 1999), 60–67.]

# INTRODUCTION

**Reading in Company**

We read with the company we keep. Reading is a community exercise, a private experience that takes place within a community.

Take the newspaper, for example. Most of us, although we look like we are reading it alone, hidden behind the first fold of the large sheet of paper, read the newspaper in company. In an election year, if we have a favorite candidate, we read the paper in the company of our political party. Our loyalty shapes how we read the reports of the political campaign. We grumble if we feel that the paper has not reported our candidate's words or actions with the enthusiasm that we feel. We read the reports of the opposing candidate with a critical eye.

At times we bring mixed company to our reading. I cannot read about the conflict between Israel and Palestine without feeling the presence of both Palestinian and Jewish friends. I feel their heartbreak. I grieve the tragedies that both sides of the conflict bear.

We also keep company when we read the Bible. The Bible has been around so long that it does not come to us unaccompanied. That is a mixed blessing because we can unwittingly bring others with us to the Bible, and our negative associations with them can inhibit our experience of scripture. We can be free, however, to choose the company we keep when we approach the Bible. One step to that freedom is to become aware of just who our reading companions are. Otherwise our way of reading is simply an unconscious habit, rather than an expression of freedom.

Self-awareness is especially valuable in the spiritual life because it can bring us into fuller contact with our humanness and with the God with whom we aspire to be in relationship. In the eighth chapter of the Acts of the Apostles, the apostle Philip is led by the Spirit to run to catch up with a chariot, where he hears an official of the Ethiopian court reading from the prophet Isaiah. Philip asks him, "Do you understand what you are reading?" He responds, "How can I, unless someone guides me?" The Ethiopian official has come to Jerusalem to worship the God of Israel. He is reading scripture, but he knows that he needs Philip, as an agent of the Spirit, to guide him into understanding.

This story is also our story. Like the Ethiopian court official, we feel a thirst for the presence of God. We undertake a spiritual journey, to approach God in worship. Yet when we pick up the Bible, we find that we need someone to guide us and to be our companion.

By training, I am a church historian, and I think of church history as the church's attic. Many houses have attics, basements, or backyard storage sheds, where we

INTRODUCTION

put things and then forget that they are there. We are heirs to an amazing legacy, but many Christians don't know much about what's in our own attic. My calling in life is to take people up to our common attic and look around and see what's there. Much of what we find in our attic we may put back into storage, but some things we may just choose to take downstairs with us and use once again. Whatever we decide to do with what's in the attic, it's a good thing simply to know what is there. After all, it's our attic; it belongs to all of us.

Because I have studied the history of Christianity, I have made friends with believers across the ages. When I read the Bible, they are my reading companions, just as people that I have known in my own lifetime, such as a favorite teacher or a dear friend, accompany me when I read Scripture. When I read the Psalms sung by pilgrims on their way to the Temple in Jerusalem, I like to have Augustine of Hippo, the great North African writer of the ancient church, as my companion. When I am reading some of the Gospel stories, I like the company of Johannes Tauler, a German mystic of the fourteenth century. When reading the Song of Songs, I like to be with Gertrud of Helfta and Bernard of Clairvaux, great mystics of the medieval church.[1] Each of these writers has enriched my understanding of scripture, so when I open the pages of the Bible I feel I have entered a great space, filled with many friends and spiritual guides. This book might have been about any of them, but the companions I have chosen for this particular journey into the Bible are the early members of my own small community in the wider Christian tradition, the Quakers, or as they are more officially known, the Religious Society of Friends.

Each traditional expression of Christianity has its own spiritual gift to offer the wider body. One gift of the Quaker tradition is its particular integration of the inward and outward life. Quaker spirituality at its best has always embraced a contemplative orientation with a social activism. Early Friends read scripture in a meditative way that nourished them inwardly yet also propelled them into human society with a zeal to reform it in a way conformable with Jesus' proclamation of the reign of God. To read scripture with early Friends is to encounter this gift. We can see this way of reading in their writings, which are filled with biblical echoes. If you are new to early Quaker writings, be forewarned that the English language has changed to some extent in the last three hundred and fifty years. You may need to slow down a bit as you read passages from early Friends, but the rewards are worth the effort.

**Writing a Letter**

Writing a book is something like writing a letter. It helps to be able to imagine who might be reading what gets written. As I wrote this book, I had in mind a spectrum of imaginary readers. Here are two of them.

On one end there is the person who has no objection to reading the Bible but may not know that the Bible has been read rewardingly in many ways over the centuries.

To such readers I hope to offer a way of reading the Bible in the company of Friends. If you are in this category of readers, it is my desire that you might explore this practice of meditative reading and discover that you can be inwardly nourished by it.

On the other end I imagine the reader who may be interested in the Society of Friends but who has some hesitation about opening the pages of scripture. There is usually a good reason for such reluctance. The Bible has been misused as a weapon by people who are too eager to read their own agenda into it. In their insistence on their own definition of getting it right (be it doctrine or morality), some religious groups have not exercised the inclusive love that Jesus practiced and asked of his followers. To hesitant readers of scripture, I invite you to imagine that the Bible is a party—a big party that's been going on for over three thousand years.

Now if you're a shy person like me, you probably don't go to a party where you don't know anyone. But if you have a friend who is going to the party, you can go with that person. Then, at the party, your friend will introduce you to her or his friends, and they can become your friends. The prophet Jeremiah, for example, is my friend because he was the friend of John Woolman, an eighteenth-century Quaker whom I consider my friend.[2] If Margaret Fell or George Fox is your friend, you can go to the party with them. They'll introduce you to the prophet Isaiah or the evangelist John or apostle Paul, and your circle of friendship will grow.

I cherish the hope that readers on both ends of the spectrum might meet in the middle. If we can read the Bible in a way that opens the door to experiencing God anew, we may find ourselves drawn together in divine love. The holy ground of scripture—holy because there we encounter God's presence—can become common ground.

**"In the Spirit That Gave Them Forth"**

Early Friends aspired to read the scriptures, as George Fox put it, in the same Spirit in which they were given forth.[3] With early Friends as our reading companions, we can discover the power of scripture to take us into the presence of God, as they did. They can be for us what the apostle Philip was to the Ethiopian official. Through their companionship we can come to understand how they were inwardly nourished by their encounters with the Bible. If we can read scripture as they read it, we may find the scriptures become, in the words of George Fox, very precious to us.[4]

Early Friends used biblical language to describe their inward experiences. If we pay careful attention to the references to scripture in their writings, we can come to understand their spiritual experiences more fully. We can appreciate the interplay of scripture and experience in their lives. Our focus here is with a way of reading scripture that is reflective, meditative, even poetic. This way of reading the Bible opened early Friends to an experience of the Spirit that gave forth the scriptures. Their method of reading prepared them for encounters with God.

As a result, the relationship that early Friends had with scripture was rich and complex. They read the Bible in terms of their own particular inward experiences, yet they perceived their world in profoundly biblical terms. Their spiritual experiences shaped their reading of the Bible, and the Bible shaped their understanding of their experiences. They did not simply read the scriptures. They lived them. For them, reading the Bible was not just an exercise in information. It was an invitation to transformation.

Early Friends were suspicious about rigid formulas for the religious life. They felt that formulas could become a mere substitute for the fresh, direct experience of the guidance of the Holy Spirit. So they did not spell out this method of reading scripture in a step-by-step way. Yet though their writings do not *tell* us how they meditated on scripture, they *show* us. They left behind hints of such a practice of spiritual reading, and by gathering these hints, we may hope to recover this way of reading. It is my hope that their way of reading may be a viable approach to scripture for our time as well, and that it may open us to an experience of the presence of God as it did for them.

## A Road Map

The journey of this book begins with a pastoral letter written by George Fox to offer comfort to persecuted Friends who were imprisoned for their faith. Examining the biblical sources in this letter shows us how George Fox found the words of the Bible to be the language of the inner life. The story of scripture is relived in the experience of the reader. To engage scripture is to encounter the presence of God.

The next chapter looks at a passage from the early Quaker Dorothy White. Her work shows us how early Friends wove a meditative tapestry of biblical images and how they saw their own lives intricately interwoven into the biblical story. The artistry and vitality of Dorothy White's writing invites us to weave as she did.

In the following two chapters there are suggestions about how to engage the Bible as early Quakers did. Chapter 4 offers an example of a contemporary meditative reading of a psalm. The fifth chapter suggests a way to engage scripture in a worshipful frame of mind in a group experience.

The next chapter considers how the meditative reading of the Bible flourished in two other groups of Christians. Medieval monastic writers practiced "sacred reading" or *lectio divina,* to use their Latin term. I chose to look at lectio divina because it bears a family resemblance to early Quaker practice and because it is currently experiencing a revival.[5] English Puritans, who were contemporaries of George Fox and Dorothy

## INTRODUCTION

White, had their own methods of engaging scripture meditatively. This chapter presents both methods sympathetically but also considers how early Quaker practice was distinctive.

The seventh chapter reflects on how reading scripture as early Friends did can enrich our lives today. This way of reading meditatively can enlarge our experience of prayer. It can offer the words we need to understand our inward experience. Engaging scripture this way can help us to heal our impaired imaginations, and it can invite us to see the world in new ways.

The book concludes with two appendices. The first offers additional passages from early Quakers for readers who find the selections from George Fox and Dorothy White appealing and wish for more. The second suggests questions for reflection and journaling.

A note on translations: in this book I have done my own translating from the Bible. When discussing biblical passages used in early Quaker writings, I have stayed close to the language of the versions used by early Friends, such as the Geneva Bible or the King James (or Authorized) Version. I did this so that you could hear the how the biblical passages are echoed in early Quaker texts. I have avoided antiquated English forms—words such as "thou" and "hath," for example—because in my experience this kind of language poses a barrier for relatively new readers of the Bible, even though these forms lend a sense of elevated language to some people who are familiar with the King James

xxiii

Bible. When translating scriptural passages for your meditative reading, I have chosen not to feel bound to stay close to these older versions but instead have gone where I felt the Hebrew or Greek took me. I mention this in advance, so that you need not feel alarmed if you look up the scriptural passages in your favorite Bible and discover that they differ slightly from what you find in this book.

[Ed. Note] You will find primary texts for reflection (indented and set in italics) throughout the book. These appear first in their entirety. Then follow portions of the same text, with comments and, often, related scripture (indented and set in Roman type).

# READING INWARDLY

The early Friend Robert Barclay, writing in 1676, helps us to understand how Friends approached reading the Bible. He wrote:

> God hath seen meet that herein [in the scriptures] we should, as in a looking-glass, see the conditions and experiences of the saints of old; that finding our experience answer to theirs, we might thereby be the more confirmed and comforted.... This is the great work of the scriptures, and their service to us, that we may witness them fulfilled in us.[6]

Reading the scriptures is an invitation to learn more about our lives. When we read the scriptures, we look into a mirror and discover that our own inward life, both as individuals and as a community, is reflected in the lives of our spiritual ancestors. The life experiences of biblical characters are comparable to our own; their spiritual conditions are ours. We are taught by the same

Spirit that inspired the written words of scripture. At times the experience is joyful; at times the lessons can feel painful. To read is to be read.

To read scripture is to realize that we are participants in the great ongoing story of God's people. This suggests a great richness of the inward life and a profound sense of connectedness. The lives of our forebears continue in us, offering us wisdom. To read scripture in this way is to claim our spiritual inheritance and to embark on a life with many layers of meaning.

## Sing and Rejoice

We can see this meditative reading of scripture at work if we spend time with early Quaker writings, paying careful attention to how they used the Bible. Let's begin with an epistle by George Fox. When we hear the biblical resonance in this letter, we can come to appreciate its layeredness of meaning. Even without recognizing the biblical sources, the letter is a beautiful and moving piece. But when we hear the biblical undertones, it is like moving from mono to stereo: we hear things, even things that may be quite familiar, in new ways. It is like moving from a black-and-white snapshot to meeting a person in the flesh: we see nuances that the photograph alone could not reveal. To read George Fox in this way can be an enriching experience.

Quakerism began as a movement in the 1650s in England, when that country was experiencing a degree of religious freedom that was taken away when the

English monarchy was restored in the early 1660s. The government enacted a series of laws designed to render dissenting groups like Quakers extinct. George Fox's *Epistle 227* is dated Eleventh Month 1663, during a time of severe persecution for Quakers. We do not know the exact recipients of this epistle, but we can safely assume that they were suffering for their faith. George Fox wrote these words of encouragement to Friends who were filling the English jails.

> *Sing and rejoice, you children of the Day and of the Light. For the Lord is at work in this thick night of darkness that may be felt. Truth does flourish as the rose, the lilies do grow among the thorns, the plants a-top of the hills, and upon them the lambs do skip and play.*
>
> *Never heed the tempests nor the storms, floods or rains, for the Seed, Christ, is over all and does reign.*
>
> *And so be of good Faith and valiant for the Truth. For the Truth can live in the jails. Fear not the loss of the fleece, for it will grow again. And follow the Lamb, if it be under the beast's horns or the beast's heels, for the Lamb shall have victory over them all.*
>
> *All live in the Seed, Christ, your Way that never fell. In him you do see over all the ways of Adam's and Eve's sons and daughters in the Fall.*
>
> *So in the Seed, Christ, stand and dwell, in whom you have Life and Peace, the Life that was with the Father before the world began.*[7]

On the surface alone, this is a very beautiful, inspiring letter. Once we begin to appreciate the biblical references in it, we see that it has layers of meaning and is even more beautiful than it appears at first. For now, let's explore just the first paragraph.

*Sing and rejoice*

Early Friends were not distinguished for their choral work, so it seems likely that George Fox is borrowing this phrase from scripture. When we hear the wider context of this reference to Zechariah 2:10, these first three words take on a deeper significance. The prophet declares these words from God:

> **Sing and rejoice**, O daughter Zion!
> For behold, I will come and dwell in your midst.

The wider context, which George Fox certainly knew and assumed that his readers would also recognize, is a proclamation of hope and restoration. Before Zechariah's time, the Babylonian empire had conquered Jerusalem and led many of its citizens into captivity. Zechariah addresses the exiles in Babylon: "Escape to Zion!" Be freed. Come home. To those still suffering captivity, the prophet promises restoration and divine presence. George Fox invited his imprisoned readers to identify with those singing and rejoicing returnees. Even while still in prison, they can know the presence of the God who dwells with them.

*you children of the Day and of the Light*

Here George Fox is referring to 1 Thessalonians 5:5:

> for you are all **children of light and children of the day**. We are not of the night or of darkness. So then let us not fall asleep as others do, . . . but let us, who are of the day, be sober, and put on the breastplate of faith and love, and for a helmet the hope of salvation.

Just like "sing and rejoice," the biblical source for this passage is a resounding call. "Light" was fundamental to early Friends' vocabulary. The central religious experience for early Friends was the experience of the Light, the divine beacon that first shows us with all its terrifying power our capacity for sin and then leads us to a sense of victory, peace, and community. In George Fox's epistle, "Light," like "Day," contrasts with night in the following sentence.

> *For the Lord is at work in this thick night of darkness that may be felt.*

The reference here is to Exodus 10:21:

> Then the Lord said to Moses, "Stretch out your hand to the heavens so that there may be darkness over the land of Egypt, **a darkness that may be felt**." So Moses stretched out his hand to the heavens, and there was **thick darkness** in all the land of Egypt for three days. People could not see one another, . . . but all the Israelites had light where they lived.

This darkness is one of the ten plagues of Egypt, a darkness so thick that you could touch it, but the faithful were spared. As with the call to rejoice because the exile is over, this is a message of comfort and hope. Despite the literal darkness of the English prisons, Friends had the Light with them, just as the ancient Israelites had light.

> *Truth does flourish as the rose, the lilies do grow among the thorns*

This phrase is a lovely weaving together of two biblical sources, Isaiah 35:1:

> The wilderness and the parched land shall be glad,
> the desert shall rejoice and **blossom like the rose**.
> It shall blossom abundantly, and rejoice with joy and singing.

and the Song of Songs 2:1:

> I am a rose of Sharon, a lily of the valleys.
> As a **lily among thorns**,
> so is my love among maidens.
> As an apple tree among the trees of the forest,
> so is my beloved among young men.
> I delighted to sit in his shadow,
> and his fruit was sweet to my taste.

The passage from Isaiah, like the one from Zechariah, was written to encourage the exiles. There was a vast desert between Babylon and Zion. Isaiah not only promises return to the homeland but also proclaims that even the journey itself will be full of wonders. The desert will bloom and will sing and rejoice—note how similar this is to the quotation from Zechariah. Here again is hope for the exiles. Here again is a promise of restoration and renewed life for those who are suffering.

The Song of Songs was for many centuries interpreted as a celebration of the love between God and the believer. The book was a favorite of mystics for describing an intimate experience of unity with God. So with these few words, George Fox has suggested both deliverance and the intense presence of God, the soul's beloved.

> *the plants a-top of the hills*

This phrase echoes the prophet Jeremiah's response to the suffering that followed the Babylonian conquest of Jerusalem. As Judah lay in ruins and the exiles were marched into captivity, Jeremiah proclaimed consolation:

> I have loved you with an everlasting love.
> Therefore I have continued
>   my covenantal faithfulness to you.
> Again I will build you, . . .
> Again you will **plant** vines
>   on the **mountains** of Samaria.
> The planters will plant and will enjoy the fruit.
>
> (Jer. 31:3–5)

༒

*and upon them the lambs do skip and play.*

Another double reference occurs in this phrase, first to Psalm 114, which retells the story of the Exodus, the escape from bondage in Egypt. The Exodus and the crossing of the Jordan River into the Promised Land after the forty years of wandering in the wilderness are seen almost as a single event, as two aspects of God's redeeming activity. Psalm 114 celebrates the natural wonders of the events: creation itself affirms God's work in freeing the chosen people and bringing them into a homeland. Like the Psalmist, George Fox had a fondness for the natural world and drew on it for metaphors for the inward life.

> When Israel went out from Egypt,
> the house of Jacob from a people
>   of strange language,
> Judah was God's sanctuary,
> Israel was God's dominion.
> The sea looked and fled.
> Jordan turned backwards.
> **The mountains skipped like rams,**
>   **the hills like lambs.**
> Why is it, sea, that you fled?
> Jordan, that you turned backwards?
> mountains, that you skipped like rams,
>   hills, like lambs?
> Tremble, O earth, at the presence of God,
> at the presence of the God of Jacob,
>   who turns the rock into a pool of water,
>   the flint into a fountain of water.

The second text echoed here is, again, the Song of Songs (2:8):

> The voice of my beloved!
> Look, he comes,
> leaping upon the mountains,
>   **skipping over the hills.**
> My beloved is like a gazelle or a young stag.
> Look, he is standing behind our wall,
> gazing in at the windows,
>   peering through the lattice.
> My beloved speaks and says to me,
> "Arise, my love,
> my fair one, come away."

With a few strokes, George Fox has hinted both at God's deliverance in times of persecution and at God's loving intimacy. As we identify the biblical echoes in this letter, we find a rich world for early Friends. We find layers of meaning, inspired by their reading and understanding of scripture. Beneath the surface of this beautiful letter we find deeper messages of comfort to a persecuted people. We find repeated references to hope for deliverance from bondage and for a return to freedom. We find reminders of the intimate, intense presence of God despite their times of suffering.

**The Language of the Inner Landscape**

We can see that this is a rich way of encountering scripture, attending to the power of the images and symbols in the Bible. It regards scripture as the language of the soul. Contemporary Quaker writer William Taber speaks of "the language of the inner landscape," and we can see how for George Fox the Bible provided the images to describe this inward country. His epistle invites us to look within and discover just how vast the interior geography is. The story in the Bible is our own story. It is relived in our own lives. We each have our own exile and our own exodus. We each receive the promise of consolation and restoration. Scripture becomes, as Robert Barclay wrote, a looking glass.

Here again is the first paragraph of the epistle. I invite you to read it once more. Now that you have heard the biblical echoes in it, how is it different for you?

> *Sing and rejoice, you children of the Day and of the Light. For the Lord is at work in this thick night of darkness that may be felt. Truth does flourish as the rose, the lilies do grow among the thorns, the plants a-top of the hills, and upon them the lambs do skip and play.*

## READING AND REMEMBERING

The spiritual life embraces more than the reasoning faculty alone can bear. So, like poetry, it speaks to us in symbolic language—not a secret code, but a means of communication in which the images bear much more than their literal content alone.

Earlier Friends did not produce much poetry, yet they did make use of powerful symbols to express the depths of their spiritual lives. Early Friends regarded scripture as having that kind of symbolic power. The stories of the Bible are powerful not only because of their literal meaning but because they communicate in what we have been calling the language of the inner landscape.

Reading scripture is a worshipful act. We must wait upon the Spirit to understand its meaning for us. Early Friends spoke of the "history" and the "mystery" of scripture. The events of the biblical narrative or "history" have a meaning to believers in the "mystery," that is, in the interior life.

Early Friend Dorothy White wrote A *Trumpet*, or, to use her full title in all its seventeenth-century glory: *A Trumpet Sounded out of the Holy City, proclaiming Deliverance to the Captives, Sounding forth the Redemption of Sion, which hasteneth. And this is sent unto all her blessed Children, who wait for her Advancement; this Message of glad Tidings from God the Father of our Lord Jesus, is sent unto you all.* The text is a rousing piece, announcing hope to the suffering faithful. She wrote it in 1662, one year before George Fox's epistle that we looked at in the previous chapter.

This was a time of dashed hopes. Quakers and radical Puritans had been optimistic for building a godly commonwealth in England under the reign of Oliver Cromwell. After Oliver Cromwell's death, the social and religious revolution dissolved. The restored English monarch and a vengeful Cavalier Parliament did not tolerate dissent with the official state-sponsored Church of England. Friends suffered fierce persecution under a series of laws enacted to stamp out nonconformity to the Anglican Church. Despite these distressing external conditions, Dorothy White and other Friends retained hope, based on their internal experience of triumph of good over evil. In spite of the outward trials and persecutions that Friends faced, the great and long-awaited act of redemption was beginning. *A Trumpet* draws freely on many biblical texts but repeatedly on the later chapters of Isaiah and on the book of Revelation.

These two texts were written to offer consolation to the oppressed faithful, and Dorothy White makes use of them in order to offer comfort to Friends. Here is a portion of A *Trumpet*:

> And now is the glory of all nations come,
> and the bridegroom's voice is heard
>    in the land of the redeemed,
> who are come out again of Egypt,
> who are become the first fruits unto God,
>    and to the Lamb.
> These shall arise in the glorious power.
> These shall mount upward,
>    as upon eagle's wings. . . .
> These shall come unto the holy mountain,
>    where the feast of fat things is prepared . . .
> Mount Zion, where the song of Moses
>    and the Lamb is sounded before his throne,
> who hath now appeared in his eternal glory. . . .
> And so blessed are all whose feet are upon the rock,
>    the foundation of God which standeth sure.
> I will make my people as Mount Zion,
>    saith the Lord of holiness,
> and as the walls are about Jerusalem,
> even so is the Lord God round about his people.
> And blessed are they that dwell . . .
> under the over-shadowing of the Almighty.[8]

Almost anywhere in this text, we could cast our nets for biblical allusions and haul in a catch so full that our boat would nearly capsize. Without becoming overwhelmed with details, we can listen closely in places while also stepping back to see the bigger picture. Let's begin with the opening words of *A Trumpet.*

> *And now is the glory of all nations come,*
> *and the bridegroom's voice is heard*
> *in the land of the redeemed,*

Dorothy White's opening words hearken back to the prophecies at the close of the book of Isaiah (66:18) that speak of God's glory being revealed to all peoples, which for early Friends resonated with their experience of the universality of the Light of Christ:

> I will gather **all nations** and tongues,
> and they shall come and see my **glory**.

The bridegroom refers to the parable of the wise and foolish bridesmaids, from Matthew 25:6–7. This parable was often understood to refer to the return of Christ at the end of time. Dorothy White understands this coming of Christ to be a present, inward reality. *Now* is the voice heard.

> And at midnight there was a cry, "Look! Here is the **bridegroom**. Come out to meet him." Then all those bridesmaids arose and trimmed their lamps.

But it is not the voice of the bridegroom himself who in the parable utters this cry announcing his arrival. The phrase "the bridegroom's voice" is mentioned in the Gospel of John (3:29), where John the Baptist speaks of Jesus as the bridegroom and of John's joy in Jesus' coming:

> He who has the bride is the bridegroom, but the friend of the bridegroom, who stands and hears him, rejoices greatly at the **bridegroom's voice.** Therefore my joy has been fulfilled.

This joy in the arrival of the beloved echoes the Song of Songs (2:12), where the lover, understood by Dorothy White as Christ, the lover of the soul, calls to his beloved to arise and come away:

> The flowers appear on the earth,
> the time of the singing has come,
> and the **voice** of the turtledove
> **is heard in** our **land**.

❦

> *who are come out again of Egypt,*
> *who are become the first fruits unto God,*
> *and to the Lamb.*

The bridegroom, like Moses in the Exodus, leads the faithful out of captivity.

The book of Revelation (14:4) uses the language of Exodus to understand the plight of the early Christians under persecution. Inspired by the same Spirit, Dorothy White uses the language of Revelation to understand the plight of early Friends.

> These are they that follow the Lamb wherever the Lamb goes. These were **redeemed** from humankind, being the **first fruits for God and the Lamb**.

༄

> *These shall arise in the glorious power.*
> *These shall mount upward, as upon eagles' wings.*

Focusing on the image of ascent, Dorothy White clusters several biblical passages. The faithful shall rise until they reach the heavenly throne. The source of the first clause may be Isaiah 60:1:

> **Arise**, shine. For your light has come,
> and the **glory** of God has risen upon you.

The second is an echo of Isaiah 40:31:

> Those who wait upon God shall renew their strength.
> They shall **mount up with wings as eagles**,

> they shall run and not be weary,
> and they shall walk and not faint.

Again, like other early Friends, Dorothy White understands biblical passages that speak of the end times to refer to inward realities that can begin in the present. Early Friends took this idea from the Bible itself, especially from the Gospel of John, which speaks repeatedly of eternal life as beginning now.[9]

> *These shall come unto the holy mountain,*
> *where the feast of fat things is prepared.*

The image of ascent continues, with the focus now on Mount Zion. The earthly Zion, beloved of Isaiah, was the site of the Temple, where God chose particularly to dwell, and where God's presence was experienced there in an intense way. Similarly, the heavenly Zion, favored in Revelation, is where God's presence is experienced. Isaiah speaks of a festival and feasting, and Revelation of a celebration and singing.

> On this **mountain** God will make for all
> people a feast of fat things,
> a **feast** of wines on the lees, **of fat things**.
> (Isa. 25:6)

> *These, I say, shall come up upon Mount Zion,*
> *where the song of Moses and the Lamb*
> *is sounded before his throne,*
> *who hath now appeared in his eternal glory;*
>
> And I saw what seemed to be a sea of glass mingled with fire, and those who achieved victory over the beast, and its image, and the number of its name, standing on the sea of glass. They held harps of God, and they sang the **song of Moses** the servant of God, and the **song of the Lamb**.
> (Rev. 15:2–3)

Here we might want to remember the text of that glorious song in Revelation 15, since it was most likely in the mind of Dorothy White as she wrote. Note the themes of holiness, glory, and the coming of all nations—all of them encountered in *A Trumpet*.

> Great and wondrous are your works,
> Sovereign God Almighty.
> Just and true are your ways,
> Ruler of the nations.
> God, who will not fear you
> and glorify your name?
> For you alone are holy.
> All nations will come and worship before you,
> for your judgments have been made manifest.
> (15:3–4)

> *And so blessed are all whose feet are upon the rock, the foundation of God which standeth sure.*

In addition to their height, mountains are symbols of strength—mighty rocks and firm foundations. The image of the mountain makes a transition from the theme of ascent to that of security.

Dorothy White uses a composite of biblical sources:

> God drew me up from the terrible pit,
> out of the miry clay,
> and set my **feet upon a rock**,
> making my steps secure.
> (Ps. 40:2)

> Nevertheless the **foundation of God stands sure**. (2 Tim. 2:19)

> One who comes to me, hears my words, and acts on them, is like a person building a house, who dug deeply and laid the **foundation on a rock**. When the river flooded, it burst against that house, but was not strong enough to shake it, for it was founded upon the rock. (Luke 6:48)

༄

> *I will make my people as Mount Zion,
> saith the Lord of holiness,*

> *and as the walls are about Jerusalem,*
> *even so is the Lord God round about his people.*
> *And blessed are they that dwell . . .*
> *under the over-shadowing of the Almighty,*

Although the original has "mountains" instead of "walls," she seems to have in mind Psalm 125:1–2:

> They that trust in God shall be as **mount Zion**,
> which cannot be moved, but abides forever.
> As the mountains are round **about Jerusalem**,
> so the **God is round about God's people**
> from this time on and forevermore.

She seems also to intend an echo of Psalm 91:1:

> You who **dwell** in the shelter of **the most High**
> shall **abide** under the **shadow** of the **Almighty**.

The psalm goes on to promise divine protection, deliverance from the snare, and rescue in time of trouble. These later lines of the psalm may well have been in Dorothy White's memory as she alluded to the psalm's opening verse.

After a careful look at this passage from Dorothy White, we can now see how the work is structured. At first it might have appeared random, but a second look shows that her text is organized by dominant images drawn from the Bible, moving from ascent to mountains to security and divine protection. This suggests much about how she read scripture. *A Trumpet* suggests that for early Friends a meditative reading of scripture embraced a free-associative play with the text, allowing the words and images from the biblical passage to remind the reader of other occurrences of the same words and images elsewhere. These texts could then comment on one another, weaving a colorful pattern reflecting the work of the Spirit in Friends' lives.

How can we describe Dorothy White's approach to scripture? Her method of reading is, like the recent book that has brought her writings back to light, "hidden in plain sight."[10] By tracing the biblical strands in this excerpt from *A Trumpet*, we find a layeredness of meaning in her writing. Exploring the biblical sources evident in *A Trumpet* suggests how she approached the act of reading scripture, as an intricately woven text. Her reading of scripture shaped her understanding of events in her own life, and her personal experiences in turn gave shape to her reading of scripture. The relationship was rich and complex. The spiritual vitality of Dorothy White's writings invites us to consider reviving this invigorating practice of reading scripture in these ways.

# Reading Meditatively

Early Friends invite us to read in their company. Their writings, filled as they are with scripture, beckon us to read the Bible as they did. How can we embrace their way of reading and make it our own?

As you practice reading meditatively, you may develop your own method for entering into the process of reading scripture in this way. Here are some guidelines that I have found useful and that have been helpful to others as they begin:

1. Enter into a worshipful frame of mind.
2. Listen spaciously.
3. Be both focused and relaxed.

First, I come into a worshipful frame of mind and spirit as I approach the act of reading. Taking my cue from Moses at Mount Sinai, I feel that I am standing on holy ground. In my mind, I remove my shoes. I find within me the place of reverence, where I acknowledge the presence of the Holy One. The distance between earth and heaven diminishes, and I enter the gates of awe. Once within those gates, I find that I can listen at a deeper level.

Next, I try to listen as I would in Quaker meeting for worship. The Bible becomes a meetinghouse. In unprogrammed Quaker worship, and in programmed services during the time dedicated to open worship, the community inwardly gathers together in an expectant silence. Worship proceeds silently until someone feels led to share words with the rest. Friends have experienced that God will inspire words to meet the needs of the gathered worshippers. To experience the Bible as a meetinghouse means that first I come to an interior silence, where I try to calm the endless chatter in my own head. I listen to the words of scripture as though they were spoken in worship, receiving them as I would vocal ministry, since they originate from the same divine source. Just as in meeting for worship, not all the words may be edifying for all people at all times. The point is to listen to find what is meaningful for you at this time.

This listening to scripture is unhurried. It is spacious, patient, and generous. As a fiddler from Cape Breton once told me, when God made time, God made a lot of it. The point here is not to read a lot or to read quickly. It is not a race in which the goal is to get to the finish line as soon as possible. Instead, it is like a walk in the woods in which we can stop and look at the flowers, ponder the shapes of the clouds, and turn over the stones to see what is there. We are not in a hurry because we are already where we want to be: in the presence of the God who loves us beyond measure. This listening is also a savoring. A friend of mine once lived near a wonderful Armenian restaurant that she would visit regularly. The soup there was so flavorful that she would ask for a small spoon rather than a soupspoon, so that she could eat more slowly and savor the experience. Listening spaciously is reading with a small spoon.

Third, to read this way is to be both focused and relaxed. We read with attentiveness and yet with openness. We read the words with care, as though we were bathing a newborn baby. At the same time we read with an openness to where the words may take us inwardly. If we can imagine reading scripture as treading on holy ground and as sitting on a bench in a meetinghouse, then maybe we can also imagine it as an adventure. We do not know where the journey may take us, yet we consent to the guide. Reading the Bible becomes an act of courage because we face the unknown. It becomes an act of trust because we are willing to go where God may take us.

We set aside our own narrow expectations because these can limit us. In a relationship of love, such as friendship or a marriage, we can be tempted to decide in advance how the other person will act or respond. Rather than being open to the real person, who is always in some sense a divine mystery and gift unfolding, we prejudge the other person. We live in a fiction because we have refused to allow the other person to surprise us with who she or he really is—which is, in my experience, always more complex and wonderful than my own limited imagination of who that person might be. In the same way, we can read the Bible unadventurously because we have already decided what the message for us is. Rather than experiencing God's presence in a fresh way, we experience only our own predispositions. About a year after I was married, an older couple came to visit and offered some wise words. "How long have we been married now?" the woman asked. "I believe forty-eight years," replied her husband. "Forty-eight years?" she responded, "Why, we're just getting acquainted!" That's the way I want to live my marriage. It is also the way I want to approach reading scripture, always open to the unfolding mystery, experiencing what God has for me rather than just my own familiar expectations.

In short, to read as early Friends did, we invite the presence of God, we sit patiently and expectantly with the words and images, and we consent to what may happen. Reading scripture this way opens us to being moved to wonder, or to grief, or at times to laughter. We courageously allow the Spirit behind the text to touch our deepest desire, which is to be with God without reservation.

So if that is *how* we might read, *how long* do we read? If you are new to this kind of reading, it may be good to begin with short periods of time to read meditatively. Fifteen minutes may be enough as a start. Continuing for too long can result in feeling weary rather than engaged.

The attention drifts away. We lose our focus. We become bored. (This is not to belittle the value of boredom, which can be a great gift in the spiritual life. Boredom can teach us quite a bit about ourselves, but boredom is not the focus of this particular spiritual discipline.) So begin with a length of time that does not tire you and leave you wishing that it were over. Find the time span that offers you the opportunity to practice both the spaciousness of this kind of reading and to maintain the relaxed focus described just above.

Here is an example of reading in the meditative way inspired by George Fox and Dorothy White. Like Dorothy White, I attempted to sit quietly and attentively with the images of the text, allowing a word from one biblical passage to remind me of others that contained the same or a similar image. I allowed the music of these passages to play together, to harmonize, and to comment on one another. As I read meditatively, I sought to allow memory, prayer, and the deep desire for God to interweave themselves into the fabric of my reading and responding. I offer what follows not so much as a model for your own reading, which you will need to discover for yourself, but as an example of one contemporary approach to reading in the company of early Friends.

For a biblical text, I chose Psalm 126. Here is a translation of it:

> When God restored the fortunes of Zion,
> it was as though we were dreaming.
> Then our mouth was filled with laughter,
> and our tongue with shouts of joy.
> Then among the nations they said,
> "God has done great things for them."
> God has done great things for us,
> and we rejoice.
> Restore our fortunes, O God,
> like the streambeds in the Negeb.
> Those who sow in tears
> will reap with shouts of joy.
> Those who go out weeping,
> bearing the seed for sowing,
> shall come home with shouts of joy,
> carrying their sheaves.

As I read the passage with early Friends as my companions, here is where it led.

> When God restored the fortunes of Zion,
> it was as though we were dreaming.

To restore the fortunes of Zion is to return from the miseries of exile. For those whose lives are restored by the return to their homeland, it must seem like a dream—almost too real to be true. When we dream, we are not in control. Things happen to us. When God restores us or releases us from captivity and returns us to our spiritual Zion, restoration comes freely. It is not in our hands. Like in a dream, it can seem unreal, yet it is very real.

Here I recall what may be the surprise of restoration. When Jacob was restored and reconciled with his brother Esau (the story is in Genesis 33), it came as a surprise. It was like a dream. Jacob may have wondered if he were in fact dreaming. He had just, as my students say, "pulled an all-nighter," so maybe he *was* dozing off and dreaming. He had spent the night wrestling until dawn with an unidentified stranger who blessed him, gave him a new name, and left him slightly disabled for life. The next morning he faced the brother whom he had cheated and run away from some twenty years earlier and whom he was now trying to appease with what looks to many readers like an enormous bribe to buy off Esau's anger. Esau, however, is ready to forgive. Jacob's response is moving: "To see your face is like seeing the face of God" (Gen. 33:10).

Jesus "restored the fortunes" of those whom he healed in the gospels. When he restored hearing to the deaf, he brought them back from captivity in perpetual silence. Speaking more personally, I am reminded of my own struggles: as I write these words, I have just recently been through eye surgery that reversed a condition that limited and threatened my sight. As a person who finds great joy in reading, I felt like I was in captivity when I could read only with great effort and limited success. To be able to read again was to have my fortunes restored. It has been like a dream.

The Bible speaks elsewhere of restoring the fortunes of Israel. In Deuteronomy 30:3–6, the phrase is paired with God's merciful compassion that will gather the scattered exiles and change their hearts, so that they can love God with heart and soul, so that they may live.

Here I'm reminded of how the prophet Jeremiah understood what it means to restore the fortunes of Zion:

> I will restore your fortunes, and I will gather you from all the nations . . . I will bring you back from the place to which I exiled you. (29:14)

> For I will restore health to you
> and I will heal your wounds . . .
> I will restore the fortunes of the tents of Jacob
> and I will have mercy on his dwellings,
> and the city will be rebuilt on its mound
> and the fortress will sit on its proper place.
> Thanksgiving and the sound of merrymakers
> will come forth from them.
> I will multiply them, and they will not be few.
> I will make them honored, and they will not be belittled.
> (30:17–19)[11]

"To restore the fortunes of Zion" brings with it the powerful images of homecoming, rejoicing, reunion, rebuilding, compassion, love, health, and well-being. Here I find myself invited to be with each of these expressions and to explore how in my inward life I have experienced the presence of God as each of these. Recently, for example, I was away from home for over three weeks. While it was hardly an exile, to come home was an occasion of great joy. To be reunited with loved ones filled my heart with gratitude. Home was charged with divine presence. Other memories come to mind, such as an evening when my house was filled with "the sound of merrymakers" (all in proper Quaker decorum, of course!), when I felt swept away by the utter goodness of life. The memory of these and other experiences kindles afresh the desire to experience God's presence that fully once again. That fullness would surely restore my inward Zion—and would be a dream come true.

> *Then our mouth was filled with laughter,*
> *and our tongue with shouts of joy.*
> *Then among the nations they said,*
> *"God has done great things for them."*

Laughter is a spontaneous response of joy or relief. Like dreaming, laughter is not under my control, at least not completely. This verse reminds me that life, in the final analysis, will not be a tragedy. Ultimately, there is hope. The shouts of joy in this verse bring to mind lines from other psalms, such as these:

> Clap your hands, all you peoples,
> shout to God with robust songs of joy.
> For God, the Most High, is awesome,
> a great ruler over all the earth.
> (Ps. 47:1)

> You crown the year with your bounty . . .
> The pastures of the wilderness overflow,
> the hills deck themselves with joy,
> the meadows clothe themselves with flocks,
> the valleys cover themselves with grain,
> they shout for joy and sing.
> 
> (Ps. 65:11)

> Shout joyously to God our strength,
> cry out  for joy to the God of Jacob.
> Lift up a song,
> sound the tambourine,
> the sweet harp with the lyre.
> Blow the trumpet . . .
> 
> (Ps. 81:1–3)[12]

As I sit with these images, I may find myself laughing or singing. The memory of these joyful moments brings me an inner joy that kindles a yearning for a fuller embrace of the presence of the God of laughter and song, the source of joy.

> *God has done great things for us,*
> *and we rejoice.*

This verse brings to memory the song of Mary from the first chapter of the Gospel of Luke:

> My soul magnifies the Lord,
> and my spirit rejoices in God my Savior,
> who has looked with favor on the lowliness of
>   this servant.

THREE • READING MEDITATIVELY

> For indeed, from now on all generations will
> consider me blessed,
> for the Mighty One has done great things
> for me,
> and holy is God's name.
> (Luke 1:46)

I find myself drawn to consider the great things that God has done in my own life. I have a fairly ordinary life, so these great things are mostly common miracles, such as the birth of my children. Early Friends spoke of the birth of Christ in the soul. In what ways is each of us called, like Mary, to give birth to Christ inwardly?

> *Restore our fortunes, O God,*
> *like the streambeds in the Negeb.*

The Negeb is the arid southern region of Israel, a forbidding desert. Streambeds there lay dry for most of the year, but in the rainy season water coursed through these beds, like the arroyos in the deserts of New Mexico and Arizona. To have our fortunes restored is to experience life-giving water after a season of interior dryness. My mind then recalls a passage from Isaiah:

> For water will burst forth in the wilderness
> and streams in the desert.
> The burning earth will become a pool,
> and the thirsty land springs of water.
> (Isa. 35:6)

This passage follows on the heels of the words of Isaiah that we saw echoed in George Fox's epistle in chapter 2:

> The wilderness and the parched land shall be glad, the desert shall rejoice and blossom like the rose. It shall blossom abundantly, and rejoice with joy and singing.

Israel's restoration brings water in the desert, as those who escaped from captivity in Egypt drank water from a rock in the desert. [13]

Like the Samaritan woman at the well in the Gospel of John, we yearn for living water that will become in us a spring bounding up to eternal life (John 4:14–15). Like the Psalmist, our soul thirsts for the living God, as a deer yearns for streams of water. Tears of longing have been our food, day and night (Ps. 42:1–2).

> *Those who sow in tears*
> *will reap with shouts of joy.*
> *Those who go out weeping,*
> *bearing the seed for sowing,*
> *shall come home with shouts of joy,*
> *carrying their sheaves.*

As I ponder these words of the psalm, the images that stay with me are tears, sowing, joy, and reaping. My mind is moved to remember passages like these:

> Blessed are you who weep now, for you will laugh (Luke 6:21).

Such reversal of expectation—such a restoring of fortunes—is fundamental to the gospel that Jesus proclaimed. This psalm can remind us of how steeped Jesus was in the Jewish scriptures that most Christians call the Old Testament.

Those who "weep now" include Mary Magdalene at the tomb of Jesus—when her fortunes were surprisingly restored, and the gardener turned out to be the risen Christ (John 20:11f). Jesus himself wept at the tomb of Lazarus, before he restored Lazarus' fortunes and brought him back from the bonds of death. Captivity, whether the historical exile of Israel in Babylon, a seventeenth-century English prison, or an interior bondage, is a kind of death. Captivity does not promote life. When God restores the soul's inward fortunes, it is a resurrection, a renewal of life, through liberation from what enslaves us.

Psalm 30:5 comes to mind:

> Weeping may linger for the evening,
> But at dawn, a shout of joy!

This tune is picked up by Revelation 7, with a return to the theme of water:

> These are they who have come out of the great suffering. They have washed their robes and made them white in the blood of the Lamb.
> So they are before the throne of God
> whom they worship day and night in
> > God's temple,
> and the One seated on the throne will spread
> > a tent over them.
> They will no longer hunger, nor thirst,
> nor will the sun strike them, nor any
> > scorching heat.
> For the Lamb at the center of throne will be
> > their shepherd
> and will guide them to the springs of the water
> > of life,
> and God will wipe away every tear from
> > their eyes.
>
> (Rev. 7:14–17)[14]

In short, we can, with the Psalmist, sow in hope. Despite the things that bring us tears, we can be confident of a harvest. The invading army that carried us into inner exile will not return to trample our crops. Our labor will provide sustenance because God will restore our fortunes.

We can sow peace, as Zechariah 8:12 reminds us. We can sow righteousness so that we might reap faithfulness (Hos. 10:12). How can I open myself to experience more fully the presence of God who frees me and restores my fortunes?

My meditative reading is only an example. The more important thing is to find your own. Here, once again, are the words of Psalm 126. I invite you to read them with early Friends as your companions. Read the psalm in such a way that you encounter the Spirit who gave them forth.

> When God restored the fortunes of Zion,
> it was as though we were dreaming.
> Then our mouth was filled with laughter,
> and our tongue with shouts of joy.
> Then among the nations they said,
> "God has done great things for them."
> God has done great things for us,
> and we rejoice.
> Restore our fortunes, O God,
> like the streambeds in the Negeb.
> Those who sow in tears
> will reap with shouts of joy.
> Those who go out weeping,
> bearing the seed for sowing,
> shall come home with shouts of joy,
> carrying their sheaves.

# READING TOGETHER

Reading in company can include the company of the present as well as of the past. As we've seen, meditative reading is an exercise of attention, memory, and openness to the presence of God. In a group, each of the qualities can be amplified, opening the way to a deeper experience for all.

Quakerism has always placed a high value on group experience in the spiritual life. This emphasis on the collective dimension of the inward life reveals itself in the Quaker practice of worship in silence. Friends who worship under pastoral leadership, as well as Friends in the unprogrammed tradition, devote some part of their time together to silent, open worship. During this time, any individual can be called by God to minister vocally to the gathered body of worshippers. Friends call their manner of worship "meeting for worship" because they meet God and one another in the silence.

"Meeting for reading" is the name I've given to a practice of group meditative reading of scripture.[15] So far as I know, early Friends did not have a practice quite like this, but it has been my experience that reading in this manner can open the way to an experience of scripture that breathes the same spirit that we saw in the writings of George Fox and Dorothy White.[16] Meeting for reading is a way of reading with others that attends to the power of the images in scripture to take us into an awareness of the presence of God. Here are some guidelines:

First, gather together some people with whom you feel comfortable entering into a common spiritual experience. Agree in advance on how long you will engage in this exercise. Allow the possibility that as a group you may feel led to prolong the exercise a bit if it is particularly moving and feels unfinished. At first, fifteen or twenty minutes may be long enough, with some time afterward for reflection.

To begin, gather in worshipful, expectant silence. When one person feels moved, she or he reads a short passage from the Bible. This person may be chosen in advance, or the group may begin without planning who will be the first to read.

The others in the group then receive the reading. They listen to it in a spirit of generosity. They attempt simply to be present to it. They attend to the images of the passage, and sit with them in quiet openness. They invite God to be present to them in the passage and to move them to respond worshipfully.

After a respectful silence, if something in the passage brings to mind another passage for someone, then she or he offers it to the group. It may be read or shared from memory. If you are sharing from memory, try not to worry too much about quoting precisely. Trust the experience.

After a respectful silence, the process continues. All seek to listen deeply to the words and allow the Holy Spirit to move in and around and through them, touching the hearts of those present. Others read as they feel led. Often, a theme develops. Sometimes two or more themes might develop in parallel. After the agreed-upon time has passed, the group concludes. It may be helpful to appoint in advance who will be responsible for acknowledging the end of the exercise. Many groups find it helpful to mark with the conclusion with a gesture, such as shaking hands among the members of the group.

Sometimes people find the idea of meeting for reading captivating, but they fear that they "don't know enough" of the Bible to make it work. It has been my experience that the group's acquaintance with scripture is always sufficient for a meaningful encounter to occur. Our memories are deeper than we realize, especially when we come to that deep place within where we allow the Spirit to move us. At the same time, it can be important to remember that the point is not to show off what you know. Meeting for reading is not a contest but an effort to listen, to experience the power behind the words that you hear or share.

Some groups have found it useful to allow for a brief

commentary on the biblical verses. Some find that this deepens the exercise because hearing the connection of a biblical passage with one person's experience can open up possibilities for their experience of connection with that reading. Others have found it somewhat distracting and prefer to have just the biblical words themselves, leaving it up to God to finish in their hearts what may feel unfinished in their hearing. Each group will find its own way with this matter.

What follows is a transcript of a portion of a meeting for reading. Reading this transcript will do little for you if you read it in the same way that you are probably (and very appropriately) reading this sentence. As you read this record of a Spirit-filled experience, please feel invited to enter into that same spirit of worship. I recommend that, if the place in which you are reading this chapter allows it, you read the biblical passages aloud. Listen to the words as you would to words spoken from the heart by someone you love. Allow yourself time simply to sit quietly and be present to the words. If some images or phrases nourish you, take time to savor them. If other words do nothing in particular for you at this moment, just quietly let them pass. If you find that, as you speak and listen to these words, other biblical passages come to mind, feel free to say them to yourself, aloud if circumstances permit. Proceed without hurry. The words recorded below were spoken over a span of about a quarter of an hour. If you can, take that long to listen to them.

Blessed are the poor in spirit, for theirs is the reign of heaven (Matt. 5:3).

My spirit rejoices in God my savior (Luke 1:47).

Peace be with you. . . . Receive the Holy Spirit (John 20:21–22).

The peace of God, which passes all understanding (Phil. 4:7).

A shoot will come forth from the stump of Jesse,
and a branch will grow out of his roots.
The Spirit of God will rest on him,
a spirit of wisdom and understanding,
a spirit of counsel and might,
a spirit of knowledge and reverence for God.
(Isa. 11:1–2)

Not by might, nor by power, but by my Spirit (Zech. 4:6).

They will beat their swords into plowshares
and their spears into pruning hooks.
Nation will not lift up sword against nation
and they will no longer learn war.
(Isa. 2:4)

Blessed are the peacemakers, for they will be called children of God (Matt. 5:9).

On this occasion, particular themes emerged: Spirit, peace, might, and understanding. At a different time, the first passage from the Beatitudes in the Gospel of Matthew could inspire a completely different chain of biblical verses, centered on other images, such as poor, blessed, or heaven. Each experience of meeting for reading is different and pleasantly unpredictable.

When we looked at the passages from George Fox and Dorothy White in earlier chapters, we saw that often a biblical quotation deepened in meaning as we recalled its wider context. "Sing and rejoice," as we came to realize, contains in it a promise of hope for exiles when heard in its original setting in the book Zechariah. The same is true for the scripture passages in the above record from a meeting for reading. If some of the biblical quotations are less familiar to you than others, it may help to explore them and their context. Then read the transcript once again and see how your experience is different.

Even if you have read the transcript with a spiritual openness, most probably you have read it as an individual. The collective dimension of meeting for reading really needs to be experienced to be appreciated. Some aspects of it cannot be captured on paper, such as the joy of sitting with others who are listening together for the presence of the Spirit who gave forth the scriptures. At times one person will quote a passage that is on another's mind but not yet uttered to the group. At other times, the verses quoted come as a complete surprise. Both experiences are delightful. I recommend meeting for reading to you and your community.

# READING WITH THE WIDER CHURCH

When early Friends read inwardly, they were participating in a tradition of reading scripture in a meditative way that had been going on for many centuries. Although in most cases they were not directly influenced by writings that were rooted in that tradition, they drank from the same spiritual source, and so early Quaker writings bear a family resemblance to those ancient and medieval writings. This chapter sets biblical meditation among Quakers in its wider Christian context, comparing early Friends with their monastic predecessors and Puritan contemporaries.

**Lectio Divina**

George Fox insisted that the scriptures could not be understood except by the Spirit that gave them forth:

> And this I was moved to declare, that the scriptures were given forth by the Spirit of God and all people must first come to the spirit of God

in themselves by which they might know God and Christ, of whom the prophets and apostles learnt; and by the same spirit they might know the holy scriptures and the spirit which was in them that gave them forth.[17]

In words that are strikingly close to those of George Fox, though preceding him by half a millennium, William of St. Thierry advised the monastic community at Mont Dieu in his *Golden Epistle*, written in 1145, "The scriptures must be read and understood in the Spirit in which they were written."[18] The twelfth century in western Europe witnessed the flourishing of a form of meditative reading called "sacred reading," commonly referred to in its Latin name: lectio divina. Quaker meditative reading breathes a similar spirit but has its own distinctive qualities as well.

Guigo II, a contemporary of William of St. Thierry who composed a guide to lectio divina, was a member of the Carthusian religious community. Guigo's treatise is known variously as the *Ladder for Monks* or the *Ladder of Paradise*.[19] Guigo's ladder has four rungs, corresponding to four phases of spiritual reading: reading, meditation, prayer, and contemplation.

Guigo described reading as "the diligent examination of the scriptures, giving it all the soul's attention." To read with all the soul's attention, we have to slow down. In Guigo's day, reading—even private reading—was most often done aloud.[20] This helped to focus the soul's attention. Try reading this paragraph or the next one aloud and see if you notice anything different. Reading aloud also engages the body through the actions of speech and hearing. We are more fully present to the text through our senses. Reading aloud honors our embodiment and so celebrates the incarnation, which was God's celebration of human embodiment.

According to Guigo, "meditation is the zealous application of the mind" to seek "the knowledge of a deeper truth."[21] Meditation was a word rich in meaning in that era. It implied thinking, reflection, and consideration. It meant repeating the text, placing it in one's memory, and learning it by heart. Readers who practiced lectio divina described it in many ways: mulling, chewing, cherishing, weighing, and loving. I encourage you to sit for a moment with each of these images. What might it mean for you to weigh a psalm, or to chew a parable, or to love a story? Medieval monastic writers also described meditation as rumination. Ruminants are mammals with four stomachs, such as cattle, goats, and deer. Ruminants chew their cud, digest it a bit, and then chew it some more. To ruminate on the Bible is to consider thoughtfully the words of scripture, wait for a while, and then ponder them again. This rumination included what they called reminiscence, a free-associative play with the text, allowing the words and images from the biblical passage to remind the reader of other occurrences of the same words and images elsewhere.

The great Benedictine scholar Jean Leclercq referred to this process of scriptural meditation by the delightful phrase "exegesis by concordance."[22]

Meditation was an exercise of imagination and memory. Since lectio divina relies on the conviction that the biblical story is lived anew in the believing reader, to read scripture and to ruminate on it was an invitation to remember one's own inward exile, inward baptism, and inward exodus.

This brings us to prayer, the third step of Guigo's ladder. To dwell on the memories of one's experiences of God is to kindle the desire to experience afresh that presence. Guigo describes prayer as fundamentally an expression of that desire. "Prayer," he wrote, "is the devoted turning of the heart to God." The move from meditation to prayer was experienced as a very natural one. Written meditations often took the form of extended prayers.

The fourth step, contemplation, was regarded as a divine gift, not the product of human effort. According to Guigo, "Contemplation is the lifting of the mind, held up to God, tasting the joy of eternal sweetness." Leaving behind the exercise of imagination and memory, one experienced an inward silence. Contemplation was repose, resting in the presence of God with a loving gaze. Contemplation was the goal of lectio divina. The medieval monastic writer John of Fécamp, described contemplation as an experience of interior calm yet heightened vitality:

> There are many kinds of contemplation through which souls devoted to you, O Christ, find delight and growth. But my soul rejoices in none of them so much as when my soul, setting aside all else, raises to you, my only God, a simple gaze from a pure heart. What peace, what rest, what joy is enjoyed by the soul intent on you. When my soul longs to see you and meditates and proclaims your glory . . . then the weight of the body lightens, the tumult of thoughts ceases, the burden of mortality and human miseries does not cloud the mind as it usually does. All grows silent and tranquil. The heart is ablaze with love. The spirit rejoices. The memory thrives. The understanding shines forth. The whole soul is aflame with desire to behold your beauty and becomes rapt in the love of what cannot be seen.[23]

Guigo summarizes lectio divina in these words:

> Reading, as it were, places the food into the mouth whole, meditation chews it and breaks it up, prayer brings out the flavor, contemplation is the sweetness itself which brings joy and refreshment. [24]

Earlier we considered Robert Barclay's words about scripture as a mirror in which we see the conditions of our spiritual forebears and discover a correspondence to our inward lives. Guigo seems to strike a similar chord:

ENGAGING SCRIPTURE

> For what good is it to spend time in constant reading, going over the deeds and writings of the saints, unless by chewing and ruminating we can . . . transmit what we read to the depths of our hearts? And thus we can consider diligently our condition and eagerly reflect in our own lives the works of them whose deeds we were so eager to read.[25]

Robert Barclay and other early Friends noted that the Spirit inwardly reveals the true sense of scripture. Likewise Guigo states:

> There is little savor in the reading of the outward letters unless a commentary arise from the heart to reveal the inward meaning.[26]

## A Meditation by Guigo

Guigo composed a number of meditations that show lectio divina at work. His fifth meditation begins with the creation of the world and then turns inward. He moves from passage to passage of the Bible by focal images, much the same way as we saw in Dorothy White. In order to lead the reader to an experience of worship, Guigo composed the meditation in the form of a prayer.

> In the beginning, Lord, you laid the foundations of heaven and earth (Gen. 1:1) . . . And the earth, it says, was empty and void, and

darkness was upon the face of the abyss (Gen. 1:2). We see, Lord, this great and wonderful fabric of the world. It is present to our senses. Through its immense beauty and greatness it does not cease to proclaim your immense wisdom and power, which are incomprehensible and eternal. And truly, although this surpasses all mortal sense and eloquence, its purpose is to direct the attention of the mind to the new heaven and earth which you declare that you are even now creating (Isa. 65:17).

You say in your gospel that "My father is still working, and I am working" (John 5:17). What is this but the new heaven and earth? For you are fashioning an earth out of the abyss and a new heaven out of the earth. The abyss is the sinner, but when you make light shine out of the darkness (2 Cor. 4:6), so that they might throw off the works of darkness and be clothed with armor of light (Rom. 13:12), you demonstrate that you have created a new heaven and a new earth. How well, I see, Lord, that the earth of my mind is up until now empty and void.... It does not preserve the beauty of its virtues and the divine image to which it bore likeness (Gen. 1:26). Therefore it is hidden in the abyss of its blindness and the face of its creator is obscured by the darkness of its illusion.

Such is my soul, my God, such is my soul: a land empty and void, invisible and formless, and darkness upon the face of the abyss. Yet even this abyss gives forth its voice (Hab. 3:10), and this deep, dark abyss of my mind calls out (Ps. 42:7) to you, Lord, who surpass all sense (Phil. 4:7), so that you might create out of me too a new heaven and a new earth.

David cried out for this, and we with him: "Create in me a clean heart, God, and renew a right spirit in my inmost parts" (Ps. 51:10). He knew that in one sense he had already been made, but now he implored that he be made a new creature, a new heaven and a new earth. "We have heard with our ears and our forebears have related to us the work which you have accomplished in their days" (Ps. 44:1). Because of this work you say, "My father is still working and I am working." For you have fashioned each of their hearts individually (Ps. 33:15), creating in them light and dividing the light from the darkness and calling the light day and the darkness night (Gen. 1:3–5). Our ancestor Abraham and so many others are reported to have been full of these days, just as those of whom the apostle said: "You were once darkness, but now you are light in the Lord" (Eph. 5:8).

O most sublime Creator, if you still accomplish this work which you accomplished in the days of old (Ps. 44:1), why then do you not do this work in my soul? My soul is empty and void, and darkness is upon the face of the abyss. Say "Let there be light," and there will be light. You accomplished this work in Lazarus and Paul. Lazarus' face was wrapped in a shroud (John 11:44) because darkness was upon the face of the abyss. When Paul was baptized (Acts 9:18), darkness fell from his eyes like scales, so that he might gaze upon the glory of the Lord when his face was unveiled (2 Cor. 3:18). These are the scales that cause my heart to sleep constantly. On account of this, the apostles also slept during your agony, for, it says, their eyes were weighed down (Mark 14:40).

But now is the hour, Lord, for us to rise from sleep (Rom. 13:11). Your trumpet sounds repeatedly. "Rise up, you who sleep, and rise up from the dead, and Christ will enlighten you" (Eph. 5:14). Enlighten my darkness, Lord (Ps. 18:28). Say "Let there be light" (Gen. 1:3), and there will be light.[27]

The similarities with early Quaker writings are noteworthy, especially the organization by focal images, the movement from image to image, and the generous invitation to the reader to enter into a spiritual experience. Guigo and Dorothy White seem to have been students in the same school of the Spirit.

Were early Friends acquainted with the practice of lectio divina? This seems unlikely, at least for most Friends. For one thing, most of these monastic writings were not translated into English at that time, and most early Quakers, unlike Robert Barclay, did not know Latin. Yet there are some interesting hints that although early Friends were not trained in lectio divina, at least some of them recognized a spiritual kinship with works that grew out of that tradition.[28]

Like the monastic texts, early Quaker writings are intended to invite the reader into a spiritual experience, in the presence of God. Then why aren't they written as prayers? Friends were hesitant to put words of prayer in the mouths of others, as they refrained from the formal prayers for communal worship in the Anglican *Book of Common Prayer* or the Presbyterian *Directory for Worship*. To pray in the words of another, without divine guidance, would be "will-worship," that is, practices arising from human contrivance rather than divine leading.[29] To quote Robert Barclay once again:

> The worship, preaching, praying, and singing, which we plead for, is such as proceedeth from the Spirit of God, and is always accompanied with its influence, being begun by its motion, and carried on by the power and strength whereof; and so is a worship purely spiritual, such as the scripture holds forth.[30]

Just as George Fox described his mission as to take people to Christ and leave them there, early Quaker writings sought to invite readers into the presence of God, where they would be led to pray in spirit and in truth.

## Other Meditative Traditions
## in the Time of Early Friends

The Puritan contemporaries of early Friends had their own practices of meditation and contemplation. Most Protestant writers did not distinguish between the two terms. Both expressions referred to a careful attention of the mind and heart to the object of meditation, a practice that should lead to prayer. The great Puritan pastor Richard Baxter, in *The Saints' Everlasting Rest*, proposes a meditation on the heavenly Jerusalem, drawing on the final chapters of the book of Revelation for images. Baxter repeatedly points out that meditation is an act not merely of the intellect but also of the emotions. The point of meditation is to stir the heart to an experience of prayer. To assist this, he appeals to the senses and the imagination.

> The most difficult part of heavenly contemplation is to maintain a lively sense of heavenly things upon our hearts. It is easier merely to think of heaven a whole day, than to be lively and affectionate in those thoughts a quarter of an hour. . . . The objects of faith are far off; but those of sense are nigh. We must go as far as heaven for our joys. . . . It must, therefore, be a point of spiritual prudence, to call in sense to the assistance of faith. It will be a good work, if we can make friends of these usual enemies, and make them instruments for raising us to God, which are so often the means of drawing us from

> him. . . . Why doth the Holy Spirit describe the glory of the New Jerusalem in expressions that are even grateful to the flesh? . . . but to help us to conceive of them as we are able. . . . Think on the joys above, as boldly as scripture hath expressed them. Bring down thy conceptions to the reach of sense . . .

Richard Baxter invites the reader to picture herself or himself in the biblical scene.

> Suppose thyself a companion with John, in his survey of the New Jerusalem, and viewing the thrones, the majesty, the heavenly hosts, the shining splendor which he saw. Suppose thyself his fellow-traveller into the celestial kingdom, and that thou hadst seen all the saints in their white robes, with "palms in their hands"; and that thou hadst heard those "songs of Moses and of the Lamb." If thou hadst really seen and heard these things, in what a rapture wouldst thou have been! And the more seriously thou puttest this supposition to thyself, the more will thy meditation elevate thy heart.

The Puritans, like the Quakers, rejected the use of physical religious images such as paintings or sculpture. But, again like early Friends, the Puritans such as Richard Baxter compensated for this outward asceticism by taking the images within. He continues:

> Do not . . . draw them in pictures! but get the liveliest picture of them in thy mind that thou possibly canst, by contemplating the scripture account of them, till thou canst say, "Methinks I see a glimpse of glory! Methinks I hear the shouts of joy and praise," and even stand by Abraham and David, Peter and Paul, and other triumphant souls! Methinks I even see the Son of God appearing in the clouds, and the world standing at his bar to receive their doom; and hear him say, "Come, ye blessed of my Father," and see them go rejoicing into the joy of their Lord! . . . Thus you see how it excites our affections in this heavenly work, if we make strong and familiar suppositions from our bodily senses, concerning the state of blessedness, as the Spirit hath in condescending language expressed it.[31]

Richard Baxter invites the reader to meditate on the joys of heaven as the most appropriate practice to arouse the affections. Other writers in that era proposed other subjects. Edmund Calamy, writing in 1680, makes these suggestions:

> Go and take the Bible and read the history of [Christ's] Passion; and when thou readest any thing remarkable, lay thy book aside and meditate seriously of that passage. As for example, when thou comest to read of Christ sweating drops of blood; that Christ in a cold winter night upon the ground for thy sake should shed drops of blood; lay thy book aside, and meditate on these

drops of blood; Oh the wrath of God that he then suffered! And so when thou comest to read what Christ suffered upon the cross, when he cried out, "My God, my God, why hast thou forsaken me!" Lay aside thy book and meditate on the love of Christ that was forsaken for thy sake.[32]

While recognizing the beauty of this practice of meditative reading of scripture, we can see some differences from lectio divina and from the reflective practice of reading the Bible that lies behind the writings of early Friends.

First, the practice of meditation proposed by Richard Baxter and John Calamy is focused, not associative. It does not lend itself to the reverent playfulness of moving from one biblical passage to another, like a honeybee in a biblical garden. It invites the use of the imagination, but in a form of concentration. In addition, Puritan manuals for meditation show a concern for structure.

For early Friends who placed great value on the spontaneity of the Holy Spirit, such structure was too stifling. Robert Barclay wrote in his *Apology* that Friends are "not against meditation," provided that it is done under divine guidance, waiting upon God, rather than some humanly contrived "thoughts and imaginations" of the willful, spiritually unregenerate person. Robert Barclay may have had in mind the highly structured method of biblical meditations of the Puritans as outlined by Richard Baxter in his *Saints' Everlasting*

*Rest.* Although early Friends most likely did not practice medieval lectio divina as such, the flexibility of the practice seems closer to it in disposition than it does to more highly structured methods.

The English Protestant texts that we have just considered also differ significantly from the Quaker writings we have been examining in this respect: the person who meditates on the biblical text does so as a spectator, not a participant. One imagines the future in heaven or the past in biblical history, but these are not held up as present realities experienced inwardly—or, to use the expression of Robert Barclay, fulfilled inwardly. One reason that early Friends did not speak so much about life after death is that, like the Gospel of John, they believed that eternal life began in this life. Likewise, early Friends reflected on the death of Christ, but, again to refer to Robert Barclay, the historical sufferings and death of Christ do not save without the inward experience, the inward birth of Christ in the soul.[33]

Where Quaker practice may be closer in spirit to their contemporary English Puritans is that both groups were spiritual activists, engaged in an effort to remake human society to conform to the reign of God. So for Quakers, unlike the medieval monastic writers, the goal of meditative reading of scripture was not contemplative rest. Friends expected to be led into new truth, to be moved into action. Inward transformation issued forth in concrete action. The biblical-image-laden texts of early Friends, they look closer to Cistercians and to Carthusians such as Guigo, but they differ in an important way. When they identified with the biblical prophets or the early apostles or Christ himself, early Friends expected to be led to behave as prophets, to engage the world as did the early apostles, and to act in a Christ-like ways to reform the world.[34]

# 6

# READING TO BE TRANSFORMED

In all true prayer, we open ourselves to being transformed. When we invoke the Holy Spirit to guide us as we read scripture, we are asking to grow spiritually. We extend the invitation for God to change us and our lives.

**The Prayer of Quiet Sitting**

One thing that can happen as a result of reading this way is that it can enlarge the way we pray. There are many ways to pray. At times we speak. At times we listen. The practice of sitting quietly with a word or image that stays with us as we read is a listening form of prayer. We might call it the prayer of sitting with, or the prayer of being present, or the prayer of waiting. It is a prayer of receptivity, of openness to mystery. As we read, we feel somehow drawn to a word in scripture and we sit quietly in the presence of God, attracted but not working too hard. It is more a matter of being willing to receive whatever gift it may have to offer, and this gift may not be revealed immediately.

At times simply sitting with a word or phrase, such as a biblical image of God as shepherd or rock or mother or eagle, seems to allow an inward work to be done in us at the very edge of consciousness. All that is left with us is a sense that some healing is taking place, but as with medicine, we may see only its effects. It leaves a sense of mystery and gratitude. Since we trust the healing power of the Spirit, we need not pry too far into this mystery. If we need to understand it more fully later, we can trust that the understanding will come. We can trust because this inner work leaves a feeling of peace and quiet joy. If, on the other hand, the experience leaves us feeling disturbed or anxious, caution may be in order. Experience has left me persuaded that the opposite of truth is often not an outright lie but rather a more deceptive half-truth that leaves confusion in its wake. Confusion is one of the major tools of evil, at least in my experience, because it takes advantage of our great capacity for self-deception. But if this prayer of quietly sitting with an image or word leaves us inwardly at peace and gently drawn toward greater love, then we can feel confident that God is at work. Then we can be at ease with whatever deep work may be taking place, however hidden it may be from our conscious understanding. Reading scripture with early Friends offers us this very quiet, restful mode of prayer that can increase our trust in God's unseen activity in the depths of the soul.

## Giving Words to Experience

In addition, meditative reading can give us language to understand spiritual experiences that we previously could not name. At times, when reading scripture in this prayerful way, we come across a word or phrase that captures something that we've been feeling but have lacked the words to describe. Suddenly, something in us says, "Yes! That's what you've been experiencing." I offer the following as an example.

In the second chapter of Mark we find the story of Jesus healing the paralytic. In that story Jesus is at home in Capernaum, surrounded by such a crowd that there was no room for anyone else, even by the doors of the house. Then four sturdy and determined people arrived and carried a paralyzed person to the roof of the house. After making an opening in the roof above where Jesus was speaking, they lowered their companion on his mat. Jesus saw their faith and healed the person, both of paralysis of body and of paralysis of soul (by proclaiming forgiveness).

I keenly recall reading this story in a time of emotional paralysis for me. I was deeply grieving the death of a loved one. Normally I'm a fairly cheerful person, but at that time I felt little joy. Death had cast its shadow, and I felt the emptiness of loss. Friends and family among the living, however, surrounded me with their love. As I encountered the story in Mark, it dawned on me that my loved ones were making a hole in the roof and lowering me down through the opening, so that I could be healed.

Their faith was sustaining me. This story enabled me to realize what was happening in my life. It gave words to my experience. As a result, I was able to rise, take up my mat, and go home. I could move beyond the paralyzing feelings of grief. To return to the words of Robert Barclay, I had peered into the looking-glass of scripture and found the correspondence between my inward life and the life of our forebears in the faith.

**Opening the Gates of Imagination**

Reading meditatively can invite us into new experiences. The language of scripture opens the door to new dimensions of the inward life. Remember Robert Barclay's image of scripture as a mirror in which we discover the correspondence between ourselves and our forebears in faith. Just as we are invited to see how the life of our spiritual ancestors reflects ours, we are also invited to consider how our lives might reflect theirs. To experience this, we must imagine.

This kind of reading opens the gates of imagination as a spiritual resource. God, who created us in the divine image, as it says in the creation story (Gen. 1:27), clearly has imagination. Part of our being created in God's image is the power itself to imagine. When misused, the human imagination can create self-indulgent and even destructive fantasies, but when used under divine guidance, the imagination can be a powerful tool for the transformation of self and society. I once asked a

Benedictine monk, whose inner life had been shaped for many years by the practice of lectio divina, about the role of the imagination in the spiritual life. "It's absolutely essential!" he replied. "How can we expect the world to become a better place if we cannot imagine it so?" Imagination points the way to new possibilities. What might it mean, for example, to be a living stone being built into a spiritual house (1 Pet. 2:5)? To what kind of inner experience does that expression invite us? Or what could it be like to feast at a banquet offered by Wisdom (Prov. 9:1–6)? (See the selection from Sarah Blackborrow in the appendix for her answer to this question.) If these particular images do not speak to you, I encourage you to find your own images that strike you and beckon you to new territory in the inward life.

Meditative reading opens a way for us to reclaim the positive use of the imagination. Prayerful reading of scripture in this way can help to heal the imagination. Our culture leaves us with impaired, atrophied imaginations. So often our advertisement-dominated media encourage us to fantasize about our pleasure but not to embrace a reality that may require us to change ourselves and our society. Reading scripture with the gates of imagination open can help to reverse that condition so that, with grace, we might undo that atrophy and courageously embrace God's invitation to grow spiritually.

## Beyond Reading: Listening to Life, Widening the Circle

Moving beyond time set aside for reading, this spiritual practice invites us to change how we see the world and how we shape our lives.

For example, after a meditative reading of the story of the raising of Lazarus in John 11, we might feel led to spend a few hours or even a whole day being Lazarus. If you returned from the dead, how would you see the world? The tremendous preciousness of this life, of this fragile world, and of human relationships may sharpen your vision. Contemporary practitioners of lectio divina call this "doing lectio divina on life." To put this in Quaker terms, just as when we read scripture we listen for the Spirit who gave them forth, so we can listen for the Spirit in our wider lives. In meditative reading we bring to the text a care, a relaxed focus, an openness to surprise, and a consent to the experience of awe. We can take these same qualities to our other daily activities, so that we might perceive the presence of God there.

As I prepare supper for my family, for example, if I approach this act with reverence and awareness, an everyday task can become a doorway to divine presence. As I cook, I can celebrate the abundance of this creation that God has given us. Putting on my kitchen apron becomes an act of prayer, reminding me that, in my own small way, I am participating in the mystery of sustaining life as I prepare a meal that will nourish my family. As I stir herbs into the vegetables, I think of the sweet savor of the evening sacrifice spoken of in Exodus 29, where God promises to be present, and I open myself to that presence. The point is not that cooking supper makes me special—or even that I am that great a cook! Instead, the point is that by approaching this daily chore with an intention to be spiritually aware, I can discover that the same Spirit who gave forth the scriptures is with me in the kitchen. Reading the Bible with early Friends has prepared me for that encounter with God by cultivating the skills for that awareness.

The same Spirit that inspired the biblical writers surrounds us in our day-to-day lives. We can listen to the words of those around us as though the Spirit were striving to break through them into our awareness. Who in your normal life speaks thoughtful words that make the gospel come alive for you? What prophets have you met? Where is God at work in what you see happening around you? Ordinary acts of kindness reveal their true nature as manifestations of divine inspiration when we give them our attention. Life becomes charged with holiness. Miriam may no longer be with us, but if we listen we can hear her spiritual daughters sing in our time. Ruth's days are in the distant past, but her spiritual heirs are among us, bringing renewed life and joy to the Naomis in our midst.

The sense of connectedness that we may come to feel with biblical stories and figures through meditative reading can grow to be applied to wider life. As we come to see that the biblical story is our personal story, we may also come to see that others' stories can in some sense become our own story. John Woolman, who lived a century after the earliest Friends discussed in this book, is a powerful example of this. As he read the Bible, he felt an intimate empathy with some biblical characters, or, to use his expression, "a near sympathy" with them. This imaginative skillfulness in connection with figures from the Bible enabled him to embrace the reality of the oppressed and poor in his own day and to feel a near sympathy with them. As a result, he labored faithfully in the ministry to end slavery, to advocate for the poor, and to call for justice for the Native Peoples of North America.[35]

As we listen to life with the same care that we bring to engaging the Bible, we may, like John Woolman, discover that our lives become widened. We feel linked to others outside our immediate circles. We may find ourselves summoned beyond the limits of our group identities. Here is an example from my life, which I offer not so much as a model to follow but rather as an invitation to consider how your life may, with divine guidance, become widened. In recent years, in part growing out of my experience of reading scripture meditatively, I have felt led to interfaith dialogue. I feel especially drawn to Muslim-Christian dialogue, since at this moment in history there is so much misunderstanding. When John Woolman felt led, in a time of war when the journey was perilous, to travel to a settlement of the Delaware Nation or Lenni Lenape, he described his urge to meet with them in these words:

> Love was the first motion, and then a concern arose that I might feel and understand their life and the spirit they lived in, if haply I might receive some instruction from them, or they in any degree helped forward by my following the leadings of Truth amongst them.[36]

His words offer a clear portrait of a near sympathy. In a similar way, I feel led, as do many others in our time, to spend time in conversation with Muslims, to listen for the movement of the Spirit in their lives. To follow this leading is to take a step toward peacemaking, so sorely needed in our day.

In the same way, as we listen to life for the presence of God, we may find ourselves called to build bridges across divisions of race and ethnicity, to participate in the effort to build a more just society. Or we may feel called to work with fellow Christians with whom we may disagree on the divisive issues of our day to explore how we may be called to a deeper unity so that we can find a way forward.

Like early Friends, we may seek to integrate the inward life of prayer and the outward life of changing society for the better. With early Quakers as our reading companions as we engage scripture, we may find that spiritual formation leads to social reformation because the God of love we encounter in reading the Bible sends us forth to love the world.

# Appendix A

# More Reading with Early Friends

Some readers may enjoy more journeys through early Quaker writings, like the ones we made through George Fox's *Epistle 227* and Dorothy White's *Trumpet*. This appendix has gathered some passages from early Friends for those who wish more. As with those two texts, here the main biblical references are noted, but the list is not exhaustive, lest the reader be left exhausted.

In the first passage, from Sarah Blackborrow, we'll walk carefully through the text, describing the scriptural allusions and how they work together. For the later passages, brief identifications of the biblical sources will suffice, so that readers can explore them and discover their connections for themselves.

## Sarah Blackborrow, *A Visit to the Spirit in Prison*, 1658

Sometimes when one writes in the first person instead of the second person, the personal intensity of the writing increases. This is what we find in the work of Sarah Blackborrow. She shows us what she sees when she looks into scripture as a looking glass, and the view is breathtaking. The source of this excerpt is Sarah Blackborrow's *A Visit to the Spirit in Prison; And an Invitation to All People to Come to Christ, the Light of the World, in Whom is Life, and Doth Enlighten Everyone that Cometh into the World* . . . written in 1658. In terms of form, this text is a prophetic proclamation. Early Friends, both women and men, saw themselves as inspired by the same Spirit as the biblical prophets were, and so like them they railed against the religious outrages of their day. Sarah Blackborrow's text is, among other things, a strong criticism of what she regarded as the religious hypocrisy of her contemporaries. But she does not stop at criticism alone. Her work is also an invitation to what she found to be a better way. So in the midst of a text in which she is crying out against those who may well have regarded themselves as her enemies, we find these words:

> *A Love there is which doth not cease, to the seed of God in you all; and therefore doth invite you every one . . . to return into it, that into Wisdom's house you may come, where there is a feast provided of things*

*well refined, and the living bread of God is known and fed upon, and the fruit of the Vine drunk of, the unity in the Spirit witnessed, the well-beloved of the Father is here, and this is he who is the fairest of ten thousand, there is no spot nor wrinkle in him; long did my soul thirst after him. . . . Now all you who thirst after your beloved, come into Wisdom's house. . . . Oh! love truth and its Testimony, whether its Witness be to you, or against you, love it, that into my Mother's house you all may come, and into the Chamber of her that conceived me, where you may embrace, and be embraced of my dearly beloved one . . . Love is his Name, Love is his Nature, Love is his life, surely he is the dearest and the fairest.*[37]

Sarah Blackborrow rivals George Fox and Dorothy White in how deeply her words are rooted in scripture. As with their texts, exploring those roots reveals the layeredness of meaning in her words.

*A Love there is which doth not cease, to the seed of God in you all; and therefore doth invite you every one . . . to return into it, that into Wisdom's house you may come, where there is a feast provided.*

Sarah Blackborrow is referring to Wisdom's house and feast as found in Chapter 9 of the book of Proverbs.

**Wisdom** has built her **house**. She has hewn her seven pillars. She has prepared her feast, she has mixed her wine, and she has set her table. She

> has sent out her female servants to call from the heights of the town, "You that are simple, turn in here!" To those without sense she says, "Come, eat of my bread and drink of the wine I have mixed. Lay aside immaturity, and live, and walk in the way of insight." (Prov. 9:1–6)

Sarah Blackborrow is drawn to the feminine imagery of Wisdom, that figure in whom God takes great delight and who is God's coworker in the act of creation, as described in the book of Proverbs.

> God created me at the beginning of God's work,
> the first of God's acts of old.
> Long ago I was brought forth,
> at the first, before the beginning of the earth.
> When there were no depths I was given birth,
> when there were no springs abounding with water.
> Before the mountains were settled,
> before the hills, I was brought forth. . . .
> When God established the heavens, I was there,
> when God drew a circle on the face of the deep,
> when God made firm the skies above and
> established the fountains of the deep . . .
> then I was beside God, like a master worker and confidant;
> and I was God's delight from day to day,
> rejoicing in God's presence always,
> rejoicing in God's world
> and delighting in the human race.
> (Prov. 8:22–31)

Sarah Blackborrow sees herself as one of the female servants of Wisdom, calling her hearers to Wisdom's banquet.

> *where there is a feast provided of things well refined*

Isaiah 25:6 speaks of another feast, a joyous banquet for all on the holy mountain of Zion. In Isaiah this is a hope for the future, but for Sarah Blackborrow it is already happening. Like Robert Barclay, she finds the great work of scripture to be its fulfillment in her life.

> On this mountain God of hosts will make for all peoples a **feast** of rich food, a feast of wines **well-refined**.

༺❀༻

> *and the living bread of God is known and fed upon*

In the Gospel of John (6:48) Jesus declares, "I am the bread of life. Your ancestors ate the manna in the desert, yet they died. This is the bread that comes down from heaven, so that one may eat of it and not die. I am the **living bread** that came down from heaven. One who eats of this bread will live forever, and the bread that I will give for the life of the world is my flesh." For Sarah Blackborrow, the feast is the presence of Christ, who gives eternal life.

*and the fruit of the Vine drunk of*

The bread and the cup were the elements of communion for those who observed the outward sacraments. Friends stressed the internal quality of communion with God. Here the source is the Gospel of Luke (22:14):

> When the hour came, he reclined at the table, and the apostles with him. He said to them, "I have eagerly desired to eat this Passover with you before I suffer; for I tell you, I will not eat it until it is fulfilled in the kingdom of God." After taking a cup and giving thanks, he said, "Take this and divide it among yourselves. For I tell you that from I will not **drink** again of the **fruit of the vine** until the reign of God comes."

In Wisdom's feast, because the living bread is present, the reign of God has *already* come. So the fruit of the vine is drunk once again.

*the unity in the Spirit witnessed*

Communion breeds community. Here we see an echo of Ephesians 4:1:

> with all humility and gentleness, with patience, bearing with one another in love, endeavoring to maintain the **unity of the Spirit** in the bond of peace

# APPENDIX A • MORE READING WITH EARLY FRIENDS

—a beautiful description of the quality of community that early Friends experienced.

*the well-beloved of the Father is here,*

"Well-beloved" suggests the great biblical love song, the Song of Songs (1:13):

> My **well-beloved** is to me a bag of myrrh that lies between my breasts.

Isaiah 5:1 may also be intended here:

> Let me sing for my **well-beloved**
> a song of my beloved concerning
> his vineyard,

which in turn brings to mind the fruit for the vine she mentioned earlier. But the addition of "Father" echoes a further biblical source, the story of the transfiguration.

> After six days, Jesus took with him Peter and James and his brother John and led them up a high mountain, by themselves. He was transfigured before them: his face shone like the sun, and his clothes became dazzling white. Suddenly there appeared to them Moses and Elijah, talking with him. Then Peter said to Jesus, "Lord, it is good for us to be here. If you wish, I will pitch three tents here: one for you, one for Moses, and one for Elijah." While he was still speaking, suddenly

a bright cloud overshadowed them, and from the cloud a voice said, "This is my Son, the **beloved**. With him I am **well** pleased. Listen to him." (Matt. 17: 1–5)

So here Sarah Blackborrow combines the sense of divine intimacy from the Song of Songs with the dazzling revelation of the real nature of Jesus. When we recognize the scriptural echoes in her text, we can begin to realize the intensity of her writing—and her experience.

> *and this is he who is the fairest of ten thousand, there is no spot nor wrinkle in him;*

Like the centuries of Jewish and Christian mystics before her, she returns repeatedly to the Song of Songs for language that can bear the weight of the experience she is trying to convey.

> My beloved is radiant and ruddy,
> the chiefest among **ten thousand**.
> (5:10)

> You are altogether fair, my love.
> There is **no spot** in you.
> (4:7)[38]

*long did my soul thirst after him.*

While maybe not interpreted quite as mystically or as intensely as the Song of Songs, the Psalms have been read quite personally by readers throughout the ages. They seem written to invite this personal identification with the Psalmist since they are so often written in the first person. Here Sarah Blackborrow's phrase echoes two of the Psalms.

> As a deer pants for streams of water,
> so my soul pants for you, O God.
> My **soul thirsts** for God,
> for the living God
> 
> (42:1)

and

> O God, you are my God. I seek you.
> My **soul thirsts** for you.
> My flesh faints for you,
> as in a dry, weary land without water.
> 
> (63:1)

❦

*Now all you who thirst after your beloved, come into Wisdom's house.... Oh! love truth and its Testimony, whether its Witness be to you, or against you, love it, that into my Mother's house you all may come, and into the Chamber of her that conceived me*

Wisdom's house from Proverbs becomes the mother's house from the Song of Songs, a meeting place for the soul and the beloved, safe from the scorn of the wider world.

> If only you were like a brother to me,
> who nursed at my mother's breast.
> Then if I met you outside,
> I would kiss you,
> and no one would despise me.
> I would lead you,
> I would bring you into the **house of my mother**,
> and into the **chamber of her who conceived me**.
> I would let you drink of the spiced wine,
> of the juice of my pomegranates.
>                                          (8:1–2)

༄

> *where you may embrace,*
> *and be embraced of my dearly beloved one.*
> *Love is his Name, Love is his Nature,*
> *Love is his life.*
> *Surely he is the dearest and the fairest.*[39]

Seldom has such a love song been sung in the midst of a polemic. The power of her writing compares with that of many medieval mystics, such as Bernard of Clairvaux or Gertrud of Helfta. Through the intensity and the artistic complexity of her language, Sarah Blackborrow invites us to step into the richness of this spiritual world, where the legacy of the Bible is no mere book alone but a living reality.

### Margaret Fell, *Letter to William Osborne*, 1657

Margaret Fell's letter admonishes her reader to "read within" and "read in thy own bosom"—fitting descriptions of the manner in which early Friends read the Bible. This letter begins with a meditation on the story of John the Baptist as told in Luke 3:1–9. This story contains the central themes of Margaret Fell's letter: trees, fruit, roots, and preparing the way for the Messiah. A central idea of this letter is inward growth. The letter discusses the struggle between good and evil in the heart. There one must cut the roots of the tree that does not bear good fruit. One must clean the house of the heart in order to see what is there. God cleans the inward plant so that it may grow. But how can we come to this inward victory in the struggle between the first Adam (1 Cor. 15) and the dragon (Rev. 12)? Margaret directs her readers to keep low, so that they may abide in the Light and in the power that comes from God, and that they may be faithful to the measure that God has given to each one (see Rom. 12:3).

> *My dear love is to thee, dear heart. Wait and be faithful to thy measure of the good word of God, which thou hast received, that with it thou may see*

*that which is contrary cut down. And the axe that is laid to the root of the tree, keep it there, that the fruits may be brought forth meet for repentance* (Luke 3:8–9). *And let the voice cry through the wilderness, that every tree that grows there may be cut down, that the way may be prepared for him, and the paths made straight, and every mountain and hill laid low, and the rough ways made smooth* (Luke 3:5). *This thou must read within, for this is the messenger that goes before him, to prepare the way for him* (Mark 1:2) *that baptizes with fire and the Holy Ghost* (Matt. 3:11). *And do keep low at the bottom, that the tree which cannot bring forth evil fruit, may take root downward and upward, that so thy growth may be true, rooted and grounded* (Eph. 3:17) *into the rock* (Luke 6:48), *unmovable, that the storms and tempests cannot beat down, that when troubles and trials and afflictions comes* (2 Cor. 8:2), *thou may know a sure habitation and portion and living strength in the Lord, and a pure peace which cannot be taken from thee. So my dear heart, low in the fear of the Lord wait, and keep the fast to the Lord, that the heavy burden may be undone, and the bonds of wickedness undone, and the oppressed may have freedom, and the hungry may have bread, and the soul that thirst may be satisfied* (Isa. 58:6–7, Ps. 42:1). *And this thou must read in thy own bosom, and so make sure and clean thy own house, for he that rules his own house well* (1 Tim. 3:2) *is worthy of double honor* (1 Tim. 5:17). *And so the candle that is lighted, put it not under a bed nor under a bushel but on a candlestick, that all may be seen that is in the house* (Mark 4:21), *that the enemies there may be kept down and under. For two nations thou wilt see in thee, and the elder must serve the younger* (Gen. 25:23). *So keep in the pure judgment, that the first man* (1 Cor. 15:47) *may be kept a servant, and the earth help the woman* (Rev. 12:16). *And so my dear heart, low, low, to thy own measure keep, that the pure plant may arise, where the unity is, which my heavenly Father planteth. And every plant that he planteth not, let it be cut down* (Matt, 15:13). *And every plant that he planteth he purgeth it* (John 15:2) *and cleanseth it. And so in the Light dwell and walk, where the purging is, where the blood cleanseth and washeth. Here is our fellowship and unity* (1 John 1:7). *And so the Lord God of life and power keep thee faithful and obedient, low in his fear to wait, in the pure belief, which makes not hate, but stands still where the strength is. And this is that that overcomes. The eternal God of power keep thee faithful, that a pure growing up in the eternal thou may witness, that so an instrument for his glory thou may be.*[40]

## James Nayler, *Letter from Appleby Prison*, 1653

James Nayler composed this epistle from the miseries of Appleby prison in 1653. His spirituality is one of stark contrasts: mere outward forms versus inward spiritual realities, night and darkness versus day and light, bondage and prison versus deliverance and freedom, and sin and death versus life. These contrasts seem to organize this epistle. In this world the faithful can expect shame, spite, and suffering—in other words, the way of the cross of Christ. Evil and death, however, do not have the last word. Glory, life, and rest await those who endure. These are not simply otherworldly realities. In echoes of Exodus and oracles of Isaiah, James Nayler's letter states emphatically that now is the time. Light and love are at hand.

> *James, a prisoner of Jesus Christ* (Philem. 1), *unto all that love the appearance* (2 Tim. 4:8) *of our Lord Jesus Christ everywhere, grace and peace be multiplied* (2 Pet. 1:2) *from God the Father, and from the Lord Jesus Christ. My dear hearts, whom the Lord hath manifested so much love unto* (1 John 4:9), *as to call you out of sin and death* (Rom. 8:2), *and the world, all the delights and pleasures of the world, which fades away* (1 Pet. 1:4), *up to himself, where is joy unspeakable* (1 Pet. 1:8), *pleasures and riches that endure for evermore* (Ps. 16:11). *Dear friends, watch and be sober* (1 Thess. 5:6), *that you may hear the voice of your beloved when he calleth* (Song of Songs 2:8), *and let not the precious proffers of the love of God be tendered in vain . . . your cries are come before the Lord of Sabbaths* (compare James 5:4), *who is your rest* (Matt. 11:29), *and he is now appeared to deliver you, and set you free from bondage, that you may serve him alone. . . . Follow your captain* (Heb. 2:10), *the Lord Jesus Christ, who for the joy set before him endured the cross, despised the shame* (Heb. 12:2), *and so entered into rest and glory* (Heb. 4:10). *. . . Mind your guide and follow him. Arise, shine, your light is come and the glory*

*of the Lord is come upon you* (Isa. 60:1), *the night is far spent, the day is at hand* (Rom. 13:12), *even the day of Sion's deliverance; Arise come away* (Song of Songs 2:10,13), *all you that love her . . . Awake, thou that sleepest, and stand up from the dead, that Christ may give thee light* (Eph. 5:14). *Come forth, come forth of all created things. . . . This is the day of your deliverance. . . . Rejoice, rejoice, ye meek of the earth* (Ps. 76:9), *shout for joy, ye despised ones.*[41]

## Margaret Fell, An Epistle to Friends, that were Prisoners in Lancaster Castle, 1654

The following letter by Margaret Fell seems to be centered on reflections on the prisoners in the book of Daniel who were faithful and received God's shelter. Images from Daniel are interwoven with other biblical threads, many of them from the Gospel of John. The resulting tapestry is a picture of divine nourishment, strength, and providential protection.

*Dear Brethren, in the unchangeable, everlasting, powerful truth of God. My love salutes you in the heavenly union. I am present with you, who are obedient to the measure of the eternal Light, which never changes, and who abides in the oneness of the Spirit, and in the bond of peace* (Eph. 4:3), *which never can be broken nor taken from you. Here is freedom, which the world knows not. To the measure of God in every particular made manifest, and obeyed, and lived in, doth my love flow freely to you.*

*My dear hearts, be faithful in every particular to your own measure of grace, made manifest and enjoyed; and in that which is eternal, wait continually. I charge you in the presence of the living God, that you do not neglect your several measures, which the Lord God of life and power hath given you to profit withal, that so you may come to receive living virtue from the living God, and be fed with the living bread* (John 6:51), *and drink of the living water* (John 4:10) *of the spiritual rock, which they drank of in the wilderness* (1 Cor. 10:4; Exod. 17:1–7). *And be subject and patient and do not look out, nor be weary, neither be of a doubtful mind, for the same God you suffer for, and by the same you are preserved, which Daniel, Shadrach, Meshack, and Abednego was* (Dan. 3). *And by the same Spirit ye are preserved, which they were preserved by. Therefore stand faithful and bold for the truth upon the earth* (Jer. 9:3), *which strikes at the foundation of all deceit and idolatry. And in the pure eternal Light of God abide, which is the stone cut out of the mountain without hands, which strikes at the feet of the image* (Dan. 2:34), *which is the disobedient part, which looked out from the eternal, and is shut out from God, [and which] the will of man* (John 1:13) *hath set up. And in that which is eternal and invisible, which overturns and brings down all foundations, doth your strength, and victory, and conquest stand, which is the condemnation of the world. And this is that which must sanctify you, and justify you, and present you pure and holy in his sight. And here is your safety, and here is your peace and joy, and eternal inheritance which never fades away. And the Lord God of power keep you, and preserve you faithful and bold to his eternal glory, to whom be eternal praises for evermore.*[42]

## Isaac Penington, *Letter to S.W.*, 1678

Isaac Penington had more opportunities for education than most early Quakers. The son of a Lord Mayor of London, he studied at Cambridge and wrote extensively. Many regard him as among the most mystical of early Friends.

Like other early Quakers, Isaac Penington stressed spiritual experience above mere intellectual knowledge that could, he said, lead to unproductive disputes. "I had rather be feeling Christ's life, Spirit, and power in my own heart, than disputing others about them." In his letters of spiritual counsel, he urged his readers to be open to that experience, so that they could read scriptures anew. "Oh that thou couldst feel the pure revelation from the Father to thy heart! Oh wait for a new heart, a new ear, a new eye! even to feel the pure in thee, and thy mind changed by the pure, that all things may become new to thee; the scriptures new (they are so indeed when God opens them)."[43]

With his considerable learning, Isaac Penington was not confined to reading the Bible in English alone. Allusions to scripture in his writings, therefore, can be somewhat more elusive, or at least not as bound to the King James Version or other English translations used by early Quakers. His letters offer metaphors that are found in many places in the Bible, and the references noted in parentheses are only partial. The letter excerpted below begins with echoes from Ephesians, not only in the direct allusion to 1:3 but also in its use of the words "mystery" and "fullness," which play a major role in the Epistle to the Ephesians. (See Eph. 1:9, 3:4, 3:9, 6:19 for mystery, and 1:23, 3:19, and 4:3 for fullness.) As the letter unfolds Isaac Penington concurs fully with the admonition that we heard earlier from Margaret Fell to "read within."

> *I have ever had a love to thee, and have many times been filled with earnest desires for thee, that thou mayst know the Lord in his own pure teachings, and travel into and dwell in the fulness of the kingdom of his dear Son; and that thou mayst be blessed with spiritual blessings in heavenly places in Christ* (Eph. 1:3). *In order to arrive here, thou must wait to know God and Christ, in the mystery of their Spirit, life, and power; and by that Spirit, life, and power, find the secrets of the mystery of darkness searched and purged out, and the mystery of godliness opened and established in thy heart, in the room thereof—Christ formed inwardly* (Gal. 4:19); *the soul formed, yea, and created inwardly anew in him* (Ps. 51:10; Isa. 43:1); *a real transplanting into his death, and a real feeling of his springing and rising life* (Rom. 6:4); *and an experience of the sweetness, safety, and virtue of his rising life. . . . This is the excellency of the knowledge of Jesus Christ our Lord, which Paul was so ravished with* (2 Cor. 12:2–4), *and counted all things but dross and dung for* (Phil. 3:8). *Now,*

*that thou mayst obtain this, mind the inward appearance, the root* (Matt. 13:6; Rev. 5:5, 22:16), *the fountain* (Song of Songs 4:15; Jer. 17:3; John 4:14; Rev. 21:6), *the rock within* (1 Cor. 10:4[44]), *the living stone within* (1 Pet. 2:4)—*its openings, its springings, its administering life to thee; and take heed of running into the outwardness of openings concerning the heavenly things; but keep, oh learn to keep, oh mind to keep, in the inwardness of life within! This is the everlasting habitation of the birth which is begotten and brought forth, bred up and kept alive, alone by the presence, power, and operation of the living Spirit* (John 3:6); *and the Lord Jesus is that Spirit, as really as he was man, even the holy, heavenly, immaculate, spotless Lamb of God* (1 Pet. 1:19)[45]. *And in this state, life reigns in the heart, and the horn of the Holy One is exalted* (Luke 1:69, Ps. 18:3), *the head of the serpent crushed* (Gen. 3:15), *yea, Satan trod under foot* (Luke 10:18–19), *by the God of peace* (Rom. 16:20); *who would have his children dwell in the sweetness and fulness of the gospel, in the peace, life, righteousness, and joy of his blessed Spirit and power. Oh! who would not desire after and wait for and walk with the Lord, towards the obtaining and possessing of these things? All the promises, in Christ, are yea and amen* (2 Cor. 1:20). *Inward victory is promised; the inward presence of God is promised; God's dwelling and walking in the soul is promised* (Gen. 3:8); *Christ supping with the soul, and the soul with him, is promised* (Rev. 3:20); *putting the law in the heart, and writing it there* (Jer. 31:33). . . . *O my friend! there is an ingrafting into Christ, a being formed and new created in Christ* (2

Cor. 5:17; Gal. 6:15), *a living and abiding in him, and a growing and bringing forth fruit through him* (John 15:1–5) *into perfection* (Heb. 6:1; Matt. 5:48). *Oh, mayst thou experience all these things!*[46]

# Appendix B

# Questions for Reflection and Journaling

**Introduction**

With whom do you read the Bible? Can you identify the people that you bring with you as you open the book? Are there voices that you would like to leave behind? If you could choose anyone, past or present, as a reading companion, who would that be? What would she or he have to offer to enrich your experience of reading scripture?

**Chapter One**

As you read George Fox's epistle, did you feel that any of the images might also apply to your own inward experience? What do you hear, now that you are aware of the scriptural echoes in the letter?

APPENDIX B • QUESTIONS FOR REFLECTION AND JOURNALING

We all face times of suffering when we need to hear words of hope and consolation. Do any of the words of this epistle work for you to describe the inward sense of exile and captivity? Do any of the images speak to you of restoration of that sense of divine presence and intimacy with God?

How can we enter that rich, image-filled inner world of earlier generations of Friends? To do as they did, we do not need to know the Bible by heart. They came to know it that well, but they didn't start out that way, and so we don't need to, either.

Here is an exercise to try, looking at some words from Psalm 63. Take in the words. Absorb the images, reflect on them, reverently play with them. See if there is some connection between them and your own inner life.

> O God, you are my God, for you I long;
> for you my soul is thirsting.
> My flesh longs for you
> like a dry, weary land without water.
> Ps. 63:1

Have you even been frightfully thirsty, figuratively or literally? If so, then let that image from the psalm connect with your experience. Have you ever been in a desert or lived through a drought? What have your spiritual deserts been like for you?

APPENDIX B • QUESTIONS FOR REFLECTION AND JOURNALING

*So I gaze toward you in your sanctuary
to see your strength and your glory.*
Ps. 63:2

A sanctuary is a holy place. What have been the holy places in your life? What has made them holy for you? How have you experienced God's presence there?

> My soul will be filled as with the riches of a banquet,
> my mouth will praise you with joy.
>
> Ps. 63:3

Take a moment to recall an especially wonderful meal. What have been your inward banquets?

Alone or, even better, in a group, read a biblical passage that is particularly rich for you in resonance with the inward life.

## Chapter Two

Read again the passage from Dorothy White's *A Trumpet*. As you read, what word stays with you? Sit quietly with that word or image or phrase, inviting the presence of God to be revealed to you through that word.

Choose a passage from the Bible that has spoken to you. Read it slowly, with great attention to the images of the passage. Do they bring to mind other passages? How do the images from these two contexts speak to one another from their differing contexts? How do they speak to you of your own inward experience?

## Chapter Three

Here again is Psalm 126, this time with an invitation to write your reflections of your experience of reading it.

> When God restored the fortunes of Zion,
>    it was as though we were dreaming.
> Then our mouth was filled with laughter,
>    and our tongue with shouts of joy.
> Then among the nations they said,
>    "God has done great things for them."
> God has done great things for us,
>    and we rejoice.
> Restore our fortunes, O God,
>    like the streambeds in the Negeb.
> Those who sow in tears
>    will reap with shouts of joy.
> Those who go out weeping,
>    bearing the seed for sowing,
> shall come home with shouts of joy,
>    carrying their sheaves.

_____

_____

_____

_____

_____

## For Chapter Five

Have you had an experience akin to John of Fécamp's description of contemplation? How would you describe your own experience?

Read again the meditation of Guigo. Can it move you to a place a prayer? Can you compose your own meditation?

APPENDIX B • QUESTIONS FOR REFLECTION AND JOURNALING

Try meditating on a biblical passage in the way proposed by Richard Baxter. What experience does this method of meditation open for you?

# Endnotes

[1] For those of you who wish to explore reading with these companions, here are some places to begin: Augustine, "Sermons on the Psalms of Ascent," in *Selected Writings*, translated by Mary T. Clark (New York: Paulist Press, 1984), 97–261; Johannes Tauler, *Sermons*, translated by Maria Shrady (New York: Paulist Press, 1985); Gertrud of Helfta, *Spiritual Exercises*, translated by Gertrud Jaron Lewis and Jack Lewis (Kalamazoo, Michigan: Cistercian Publications, 1989); Bernard of Clairvaux, *Sermons on the Song of Songs*, four volumes, translated by Kilian Walsh and Irene Edmonds (Kalamazoo, Michigan: Cistercian Publications, 1971–1980).

[2] For more on John Woolman, Jeremiah, and reading as an act of friendship, see my study of John Woolman, *A Near Sympathy: The Timeless Quaker Wisdom of John Woolman* (Richmond, Indiana: Friends United Press, 2003).

[3] Here is one among the many places where George Fox speaks of the matter: "And this I was moved to declare, that the scriptures were given forth by the Spirit of God and all people must first come to the

spirit of God in themselves by which they might know God and Christ, of whom the prophets and apostles learnt; and by the same spirit they might know the Holy Scriptures and the spirit which was in them that gave them forth." (*Journal*, 136. All references are to the edition of George Fox's *Journal* by John L. Nickalls [London: Religious Society of Friends, 1952].)

4   When accused of not valuing the Bible very highly, George Fox responded, "Yet I had no slight esteem of the Holy Scriptures, but they were very precious to me, for I was in that Spirit by which they were given forth." *Journal*, 34.

5   For some contemporary guides to lectio divina, see M. Basil Pennington, *Lectio Divina: The Ancient Practice of Praying the Scriptures* (New York: Crossroad, 1998); Thelma Hall, *Too Deep for Words: Rediscovering Lectio Divina* (Mahwah, New Jersey: Paulist, 1988); and Michael Casey, *Sacred Reading: The Ancient Art of Lectio Divina* (Liguori, Missouri: Liguori Publications, 1996).

6   Robert Barclay, *Apology for True Christian Divinity*, London, 1678 and many reprintings, Proposition 3: Section 5.

7   George Fox, *Epistle 227*, in *The Power of the Lord Is Over All: The Pastoral Letters of George Fox*, T. Canby Jones, editor, (Richmond, Indiana: Friends United Press, 1989) 185–86.

8   Dorothy White, *A TRUMPET Sounded out of the HOLY*

CITY, *proclaiming Deliverance to the Captives, Sounding forth the Redemption of SION, which hasteneth* . . . (1662), from *Hidden in Plain Sight: Quaker Women's Writings 1650–1700*, edited by Mary Garman, Judith Applegate, Margaret Benefiel, and Dortha Meredith (Wallingford, Pennsylvania: Pendle Hill, 1996), 147–148, with some modernization of orthography.

9 See, for example, John 8:51, 5:34, 6:40, 11:25–26.

10 I've taken this phrase from the title of the book that has brought Dorothy White back into light: *Hidden in Plain Sight: Quaker Women's Writings 1650–1700*, edited by Mary Garman, Judith Applegate, Margaret Benefiel, and Dortha Meredith (Wallingford, Pennsylvania: Pendle Hill, 1996).

11 See also Jer. 33:10–11.

12 For more examples of joyous outburst, try Isa. 12:5, 42:10, 48:20.

13 See Exod. 17:1–7, echoed in Ps. 114, which we also saw in the discussion of George Fox's epistle.

14 Scriptural echoes abound in this passage from Rev. 7, including Isa. 49:10; Ps. 121:6; Ps. 23:1–2; Ezek. 34:23; John 4:10 and 7:37; and Isa. 25:8. It is almost as if John, the author of Revelation, read scripture with George Fox—or, more precisely, that George Fox sat at the feet of John.

15 For a valuable but different approach to reading the Bible together in a Quaker way, see the pamphlet by Joanne and Larry Spears, *Friendly Bible Study* (Philadelphia: Friends General Conference, 1990).

[16] Since my own initial work with meetings for reading, I have learned that among the branch of Quakers known as Conservative Friends there is a practice called "scripture reading," in which persons gather and read from the Bible, with periods of devotional silence between readings. As it has been explained to me, and as I have experienced that practice, there is not the same focused attention on images in the biblical passages. There is not the same expectation that a key word or image from one passage might spark a series of scriptural quotations that have a common theme. Although "scripture reading" differs from "meeting for reading," it is a worthwhile devotional practice in its own right, and I commend it to interested readers.

[17] *The Journal of George Fox*, 136.

[18] *Epistola aurea ad fratres de Monte-Dei*, in J. P. Migne, *Patrologia Latina* (Paris, 1862), Volume 184, Column 237 (my translation from the Latin). Because William of St. Thierry's *Golden Epistle* was not available in English in George Fox's day, it seems unlikely that he would have known the text.

[19] An English translation is available: Guigo II, Prior of the Grand Chartreuse, *The Ladder of Monks and Twelve Meditations*, edited and translated by James Walsh and Edmund Colledge (Kalamazoo, Michigan: Cistercian Publications, 1978).

[20] Here I am reminded of the description in John Woolman's *Journal* of his family sitting together

reading the Bible aloud in the afternoons after attending meeting for worship on First Day mornings. See John Woolman, *The Journal and Major Essays of John Woolman*, ed. Phillips P. Moulton (Oxford: Oxford University Press, 1971; reprinted Richmond, Indiana: Friends United Press, 1989), 23, 28.

[21] Guigo's descriptions of the four phases of lectio divina are taken from his *Scala Paradisi*, i, ii (my translation from the text found at <http://ww.chartreux.org/textes/latin/scala.html>).

[22] Jean Leclercq, *The Love of Learning and the Desire for God: A Study of Monastic Culture* (original *L'Amour des lettres et le désir de Dieu: initiation aux auteurs monastiques du moyen âge*, Paris: Cerf, 1957), transl. Catherine Misrahi (New York: Fordham University Press, 1977), 95.

[23] Jean Leclercq and Jean-Paul Bonnes, *Jean de Fécamp: un maître de la vie spirituelle au Xie siècle* (Paris: J. Vrin, 1946), p. 182 (my translation from the Latin).

[24] Guigo, *Scala Paradisi*, i, ii.

[25] Guigo, *Scala Paradisi*, xi.

[26] Guigo, *Scala Paradisi*, vi.

[27] Guigo's guide to lectio divina, the *Ladder of Paradise*, has been well known through the centuries, though the work was often attributed to other writers, such as Bernard of Clairvaux or Augustine of Hippo. His *Meditations* had all but faded from historical memory and survived in only a few manuscripts. They were first brought to light in modern times by André

Wilmart in his *Auteurs spirituels et textes dévots du moyen âge latin* (Paris: Bloud et Gay, 1932, 217-260, see esp. 226-230). An edition of the *Meditations* first appeared in 1932, edited by M.-M. Davy, "De l'imitation de Jésus-Christ. Meditations de Guigues II le Chartreux" (*Supplément á La vie spirituelle, etudes et documents*, vol. 33). A second critical edition of these Latin texts was published by Edmund College and James Walsh in Guiges II le Chartreux, *Lettre sur la vie contemplative et Douze Méditations*, critical edition of the Latin text by Edmund Colledge and James Walsh, *Sources chrètiennes* 163 (Paris: Cerf, 1980). For my translation, I have drawn on both editions.

[28] In 1693 William Penn wrote a letter to John Rhodes in which he lists the volumes "most valuable for a moderate library." [Allen C. Thomas "William Penn on the Choice of Books," *Bulletin of the Friends Historical Society* 4, 1 (Third Month 1911), 33–42.] Among them he lists "Austin, . . . his Soliloquies," "Austin" being Augustine of Hippo, the great North African thinker of the early church. Augustine did compose a work known as his *Soliloquies*, but this was not in print in English in Penn's day. What was in print was a pseudonymous work which, according to Jean Leclercq, was usually bound with another work erroneously attributed to Augustine known as the *Meditations of St. Augustine*. This text drew heavily on the writings of John of Fécamp, a monk and abbot from the late-tenth and early-eleventh centuries. John

of Fécamp was an important forerunner of the great flowering of monastic literature in the age of William of St. Thierry and Guigo the Carthusian, and he was an important contributor to the development of lectio divina. William Penn was not aware of this, of course, but it is nonetheless revealing that when asked to recommend some spiritually edifying books, he felt close to a book that grows out of the tradition of lectio divina. [Jean Leclercq, *Love of Learning*, 76. See also his "Ecrits spirituelles de l'école de Jean de Fécamp," *Analecta Monastica*, fasc, xx, 117–123.]

29  The expression "will-worship" is from Col. 2:23 in the King James Version.

30  *Apology*, Proposition 12, Section 28.

31  Richard Baxter, *The Saints' Everlasting Rest*, Chapter 15. Many editions of this text are available. This quotation is from the website: <http://www.reformed.org/documents/saintsrest/saints_rest15.html>.

32  Edmund Calamy, *The Art of Divine Meditation, or A Discourse on the Nature, Necessity, and Excellency thereof. With Motives to, and Rules for the better performance of that most Important Christian Duty* (London, 1680).

33  *Apology*, Proposition 7, Section 4.

34  Of course, not all monastics stayed aloof from society. Bernard of Clairvaux, for example, was very active in the issues of his day, from advising the papacy to preaching in support of the crusades. In our era, numerous monastic voices have advocated for greater social justice.

[35] I discuss this more fully in *A Near Sympathy: The Timeless Quaker Wisdom of John Woolman* (Richmond, Indiana: Friends United Press, 2003).

[36] *The Journal and Major Essays of John Woolman*, edited by Phillips P. Moulton (New York: Oxford University Press, 1971; reprinted Richmond, IN: Friends United Press, 1989) 127.

[37] *Hidden in Plain Sight: Quaker Women's Writings 1650–1700*, edited by Mary Garman, Judith Applegate, Margaret Benefiel, and Dortha Meredith (Wallingford, Pennsylvania: Pendle Hill, 1996), 49, 55.

[38] "No spot" from the Song of Songs seems to have been amplified in her mind by the expression from Eph. 5:27, "without a spot or wrinkle."

[39] Given her attraction to the Song of Songs, we may have here an echo of 2:6:

> O that his left hand were under my head, and that his right hand **embraced** me!

In the Song of Songs, the lovers frequently call one another "fair" and "fairest": 1:8, 1:15, 1:16, 2:10, 2:13, 4:1, 5:9, 6:1, 6:10, 7:6. As for conjunctions of "love," "name," and "life," here are some possible sources:

> Because your **love** is better than life,
> my lips will praise you.
> So I will bless you as long as I live.
> In your **name** I will lift up my hands.
> (Ps. 63:3)

> Let him kiss me with the kisses of his mouth.
> For your **love** is better than wine,

> The scent of your oils is fragrant.
> Your **name** is ointment poured out,
> therefore the maidens **love** you.
>
> (Song of Songs 1:2)
>
> I made your **name** known to them, and I will make it known, so that the **love** with which you have **loved** me may be in them, and so that I myself may be in them.
>
> (John 17:26)

[40] This version of the text is taken from Letter 73 in *Undaunted Zeal: The Letters of Margaret Fell*, edited and introduced by Elsa F. Glines (Richmond, Indiana: Friends United Press, 2003), 241–242.

[41] James Nayler, "Letter from Appleby Prison, February 1653," from Geoffrey F. Nuttall, "The Letters of James Nayler," in *The Lamb's War: Quaker Essays to Honor Hugh Barbour*, edited by Michael L. Birkel and John W. Newman (Richmond, Indiana: Earlham College Press, 1992), 46–47.

[42] This version of the text is taken from the Digital Quaker Collection at the website of the Earlham School of Religion. I have modernized the spelling and the punctuation somewhat. The text also appears in Letter 29 in *Undaunted Zeal: The Letters of Margaret Fell*, edited and introduced by Elsa F. Glines (Richmond, Indiana: Friends United Press, 2003), 98–99, and in *Hidden in Plain Sight: Quaker Women's Writings 1650–1700*, edited by Mary Garman, Judith Applegate, Margaret Benefiel, and Dortha Meredith (Wallingford, Pennsylvania: Pendle Hill, 1996), 462.

[43] Isaac Penington, *Letters of Isaac Penington* (London: John and Arthur Arch, 1828), 171.

[44] This reference to 1 Cor. 10:4 may be the clearest allusion, since "rock" follows "fountain," but it is only one of many. See also Exod. 17:1–7; Deut. 32:4; 1 Sam. 2:2; Ps. 18:2, 18:31, 18:46, 95:1 (and elsewhere in the Psalms); and Matt. 7:24.

[45] See also John 1:29 and 1:36, and throughout Revelation: 5:6, 5:8, 5:12–13, 7:9–10, 14:1–4, 17:14, 19:7–9, 22:1–3, and elsewhere.

[46] Isaac Penington, *Letters of Isaac Penington* (London: John and Arthur Arch, 1828), 122–124.

# Scripture Index

**Genesis**
1:1 . . . . . . . . . 54
1:2 . . . . . . . . . 55
1:3 . . . . . . . . . 57
1:3-5 . . . . . . . 56
1:26 . . . . . . . . 55
1:27 . . . . . . . . 68
3:8 . . . . . . . . . 93
3:15 . . . . . . . . 93
25:23 . . . . . . . 87
33:10 . . . . . . . 31

**Exodus**
10:21 . . . . . . . . 5
17:1-7 . . . . . . . 90, 111, 118

**Deuteronomy**
30:3-6 . . . . . . . 31
32:4 . . . . . . . . 118

**1 Samuel**
2:2 . . . . . . . . . 118

**Psalms**
16:11 . . . . . . . . 88
18:2 . . . . . . . . . 118
18:3 . . . . . . . . . 93
18:28 . . . . . . . . 57
18:31 . . . . . . . . 118
18:46 . . . . . . . . 118
23:1-2 . . . . . . . 111
30:5 . . . . . . . . . 37
33:15 . . . . . . . . 56
40:2 . . . . . . . . . 21
42:1 . . . . . . . . . 83, 86
42:1-2 . . . . . . . 36
42:7 . . . . . . . . . 56
44:1 . . . . . . . . . 56
47:1 . . . . . . . . . 33
51:10 . . . . . . . . 56, 92
63:1 . . . . . . . . . 83, 98
63:2 . . . . . . . . . 99
63:3 . . . . . . . . . 100, 116
65:11 . . . . . . . . 34
76:9 . . . . . . . . . 89
81:1-3 . . . . . . . 34
91:1 . . . . . . . . . 22
95:1 . . . . . . . . . 118

**Psalms** continued
114 . . . . . . . . . . . 8-9, 111
121:6 . . . . . . . . . 111
125:1-2 . . . . . . . . 22
126 . . . . . . . . . 29-30, 33-36, 39, 103

**Proverbs**
8:22-31 . . . . . . . . 78
9:1-6 . . . . . . . . . . 69, 77-78

**Song of Songs**
1:2 . . . . . . . . . . . 117
1:8 . . . . . . . . . . . 116
1:13 . . . . . . . . . . 81
1:15 . . . . . . . . . . 116
1:16 . . . . . . . . . . 116
2:1 . . . . . . . . . . . 6-7
2:6 . . . . . . . . . . . 116
2:8 . . . . . . . . . . . 9, 88
2:10 . . . . . . . . . . 89, 116
2:12 . . . . . . . . . . 17
2:13 . . . . . . . . . . 89, 116
4:1 . . . . . . . . . . . 116
4:7 . . . . . . . . . . . 82
4:15 . . . . . . . . . . 93
5:9 . . . . . . . . . . . 116
5:10 . . . . . . . . . . 82
6:1 . . . . . . . . . . . 116
6:10 . . . . . . . . . . 116
7:6 . . . . . . . . . . . 116
8:1-2 . . . . . . . . . . 84

**Isaiah**
2:4 . . . . . . . . . . . 45
5:1 . . . . . . . . . . . 81
11:1-2 . . . . . . . . . 45
12:5 . . . . . . . . . . 111
25:6 . . . . . . . . . . 19, 79
25:8 . . . . . . . . . . 111
35:1 . . . . . . . . . . 6
35:6 . . . . . . . . . . 35
40:31 . . . . . . . . . 18
42:10 . . . . . . . . . 111
43:1 . . . . . . . . . . 92
48:20 . . . . . . . . . 111
49:10 . . . . . . . . . 111
58:6-7 . . . . . . . . . 86
60:1 . . . . . . . . . . 18, 88
65:17 . . . . . . . . . 55
66:18 . . . . . . . . . 16

**Jeremiah**
9:3 . . . . . . . . . . . 90
17:3 . . . . . . . . . . 93
29:14 . . . . . . . . . 32
30:17-19 . . . . . . . 32
31:3-5 . . . . . . . . . 8
31:33 . . . . . . . . . 93
33:10-11 . . . . . . . 111

**Ezekiel**
34:23 . . . . . . . . . 111

# SCRIPTURE INDEX

**Daniel**
2:34 . . . . . . . . . . 90
3 . . . . . . . . . . . 90

**Hosea**
10:12 . . . . . . . . 38

**Habakkuk**
3:10 . . . . . . . . . . 55

**Zechariah**
2:10 . . . . . . . . . . 4
4:6 . . . . . . . . . . . 45
8:12 . . . . . . . . . . 38

**Matthew**
3:11 . . . . . . . . . . 86
5:3 . . . . . . . . . . . 45
5:9 . . . . . . . . . . . 45
5:48 . . . . . . . . . . 94
7:24 . . . . . . . . . . 118
11:29 . . . . . . . . . 88
13:6 . . . . . . . . . . 93
15:13 . . . . . . . . . 87
17:1-5 . . . . . . . . 81-82
25:6-7 . . . . . . . . 16

**Mark**
1:2 . . . . . . . . . . . 86
4:21 . . . . . . . . . . 86
14:40 . . . . . . . . 57

**Luke**
1:46 . . . . . . . . . . 35
1:47 . . . . . . . . . . 45
1:69 . . . . . . . . . . 93
3:1-9 . . . . . . . . . 85
3:5 . . . . . . . . . . . 86
3:8-9 . . . . . . . . . 86
6:21 . . . . . . . . . . 37
6:48 . . . . . . . . . . 21, 86
10:18-19 . . . . . . 93
22:14 . . . . . . . . . 80

**John**
1:13 . . . . . . . . . . 90
1:29 . . . . . . . . . . 118
1:36 . . . . . . . . . . 118
3:6 . . . . . . . . . . . 93
3:29 . . . . . . . . . . 17
4:10 . . . . . . . . . . 90, 111
4:14 . . . . . . . . . . 93
4:14-15 . . . . . . . 36
5:17 . . . . . . . . . . 55
5:34 . . . . . . . . . . 111
6:40 . . . . . . . . . . 111
6:48 . . . . . . . . . . 79
6:51 . . . . . . . . . . 90
7:37 . . . . . . . . . . 111
8:51 . . . . . . . . . . 111
11:1-44 . . . . . . . 70
11:25-26 . . . . . . 111
11:44 . . . . . . . . . 56
15:1-5 . . . . . . . . 94
15:2 . . . . . . . . . . 87

**John** continued
17:26 . . . . . . . . . 117
20:11f. . . . . . . . . 37
20:21-22 . . . . . . . 45

**Acts of the Apostles**
8:26-40 . . . . . . . . xvi
9:18 . . . . . . . . . . 57

**Romans**
6:4 . . . . . . . . . . . 92
8:2 . . . . . . . . . . . 88
12:3 . . . . . . . . . . 85
13:11 . . . . . . . . . 57
13:12 . . . . . . . . . 55, 89
16:20 . . . . . . . . . 93

**1 Corinthians**
10:4 . . . . . . . . . . 90, 93, 118
15:47 . . . . . . . . . 87

**2 Corinthians**
1:20 . . . . . . . . . . 93
3:18 . . . . . . . . . . 57
4:6 . . . . . . . . . . . 55
5:17 . . . . . . . . . . 93
8:2 . . . . . . . . . . . 86
12:2-4 . . . . . . . . . 92

**Galatians**
4:19 . . . . . . . . . . 92
6:15 . . . . . . . . . . 93

**Ephesians**
1:3 . . . . . . . . . . . 92
1:9 . . . . . . . . . . . 92
1:23 . . . . . . . . . . 92
3:4 . . . . . . . . . . . 92
3:9 . . . . . . . . . . . 92
3:17 . . . . . . . . . . 86
3:19 . . . . . . . . . . 92
4:1 . . . . . . . . . . . 80
4:3 . . . . . . . . . . . 89, 92
5:8 . . . . . . . . . . . 56
5:14 . . . . . . . . . . 57, 89
5:27 . . . . . . . . . . 116
6:19 . . . . . . . . . . 92

**Philippians**
3:8 . . . . . . . . . . . 92
4:7 . . . . . . . . . . . 45, 56

**Colossians**
2:23 . . . . . . . . . . 115

**1 Thessalonians**
5:5 . . . . . . . . . . . 5
5:6 . . . . . . . . . . . 88

**1 Timothy**
3:2 . . . . . . . . . . . 86
5:17 . . . . . . . . . . 86

## 2 Timothy
2:19 . . . . . . . . . . 21
4:8 . . . . . . . . . . . 88

## Philemon
1 . . . . . . . . . . . . 88

## Hebrews
2:10 . . . . . . . . . . 88
4:10 . . . . . . . . . . 88
6:1 . . . . . . . . . . . 94
12:2 . . . . . . . . . . 88

## James
5:4 . . . . . . . . . . . 88

## 1 Peter
1:4 . . . . . . . . . . . 88
1:8 . . . . . . . . . . . 88
1:19 . . . . . . . . . . 93
2:4 . . . . . . . . . . . 93
2:5 . . . . . . . . . . . 69

## 2 Peter
1:2 . . . . . . . . . . . 88

## 1 John
1:7 . . . . . . . . . . . 87
4:9 . . . . . . . . . . . 88

## Revelation
3:20 . . . . . . . . . . 93
5:5 . . . . . . . . . . . 93
5:6 . . . . . . . . . . . 118
5:8 . . . . . . . . . . . 118
5:12-13 . . . . . . . . 118
7:9-10 . . . . . . . . . 118
7:14-17 . . . . . . . . 38
12:16 . . . . . . . . . 87
14:1-4 . . . . . . . . . 118
14:4 . . . . . . . . . . 18
15:2-3 . . . . . . . . . 20
15:3-4 . . . . . . . . . 20
17:14 . . . . . . . . . 118
19:7-9 . . . . . . . . . 118
21:6 . . . . . . . . . . 93
22:1-3 . . . . . . . . . 118
22:16 . . . . . . . . . 93